GHOST INVESTIGATOR

Volume 6:
Dark Shadows

Written by
Linda Zimmermann

A Spirited Books Publication

Also by Linda Zimmermann

Bad Astronomy
Forging A Nation
Civil War Memories
Ghosts of Rockland County
Haunted Hudson Valley
More Haunted Hudson Valley
Haunted Hudson Valley III
A Funny Thing Happened on the Way to Gettysburg
Rockland County: Century of History
Mind Over Matter
Home Run
Ghost Investigator, Volume 1: Hauntings of the Hudson Valley
Ghost Investigator, Volume 2: From Gettysburg, PA to Lizzie Borden, AX
Ghost Investigator, Volume 3
Dead Center
Rockland County Scrapbook
Ghost Investigator, Volume 4: Ghosts of New York and New Jersey
Ghost Investigator, Volume 5: From Beyond the Grave
Ghosts of Rockland County Collected Stories Edition

The author is always looking for new ghost stories. If you would like to share a haunting experience go to:

www.ghostinvestigator.com

Or write to:

Linda Zimmermann
P.O. Box 192
Blooming Grove, NY 10914

Or send email to:

linda@gotozim.com

Ghost Investigator: Volume 6
Copyright © 2006 Linda Zimmermann

All rights reserved. This book may not be reproduced in whole or in part without permission.

ISBN: 0-9712326-8-7

CONTENTS

Creepy Canada	1
Alterations	8
The Evil Men Do	13
Ghost Hunting Merit Badge	32
Gomez Mill House	51
Rolling Hills Asylum	64
Ghost Briefs	94

Introduction

The struggle between the living and the dead goes on, which is no surprise as it appears that the living can't even get along amongst themselves. Around the world there's death and destruction, terrible natural disasters, everything is too expensive, and no one seems to have any answers. Guess what? Welcome to life on earth as it's been since civilization first began.

Even with all of this, I choose to remain optimistic overall. Yes, there are many days that I want to pick up my life's marbles and not play anymore, but the game must go on. And as I regularly come into contact with all manner of unhappy and angry spirits, I increasingly realize the importance of enjoying that game as much as possible. I've said it before—I have no intention of being on my deathbed with a long list of regrets.

Perhaps this is a somewhat morbid introduction, but hey, it's a ghost book! You can't help getting philosophical about life the more you encounter death. This book contains cases involving spirits trapped at locations by tragedies, regrets, unfinished business, anger and just plain evil. It's not a happy bunch of ghosts, and they are not making the living too happy, either, with all of their paranormal meddling in human affairs.

By all means, do everything you can to keep the people in your life happy—but don't forget yourself! Far too many people don't value their own happiness, and their lives become endless cycles of doing what they think they have to do, not what they want to do. And the next thing you know, these people will die with a heap of regrets, become ghosts and I'll be writing about them some day…

But seriously, have fun, do what's right for you, and you'll find it usually all works out in the end.

In the meantime, I hope you enjoy this latest book in the *Ghost Investigator* series. I may be slightly biased, but I think it has some truly amazing cases of the paranormal. It also has what I consider to be the best "ghost photo" I've ever taken. And please feel free to contact me with comments and stories, as believe it or not, I still prefer being contacted by the living…

Linda Zimmermann
August 30, 2006

Creepy Canada

In the summer of 2005, I was contacted by a producer of *Creepy Canada*, a popular ghost/paranormal show that had completed two successful seasons. For season three, they were looking to go south of the border for some creepy American ghost stories. The producer wanted to know two things—did I know of any good ghost stories in the Hudson Valley, and was I at all interested in taking part in a live investigation for the show?

Of course, I had several books full of fascinating stories to share, but there was a catch. As the show was aired on Outdoor Life Network, all of the stories had to have an outdoor slant. Naturally, one of the many haunted cemeteries first came to mind, but they were looking for something different, something beyond the typical cemetery story.

"How about a house where the owner brought home a pair of cemetery gates and all hell broke loose?" I asked, thinking of the home of Roxanne Wentworth that I wrote about in *Ghost Investigator Volume 3*. I went on to briefly describe the situation and there was definite interest. I forwarded Roxanne's contact information, and agreed to a live investigation if everything could be arranged.

Everything did work out, and a shooting date was set for the fall. It was a Saturday, and my husband, Bob, and I arrived at the house in the late afternoon. Director Bill Burke and his crew had already been shooting for hours, and it looked as though it was going to be just another typical 16-hour day for them.

An actor had been hired to play the phantom man who climbed the stairs and attacked Roxanne the night the gates were installed, and it was amusing to watch him repeatedly climb the stairs with a menacing look, then chat pleasantly with us between takes. Although we could not see the attack scene, we heard Roxanne yelling with conviction, so we knew it was going to be a great segment. Of course, it was all a bit surreal—reenacting haunted activity that was all too real to the people who had experienced it.

Next came the reenactment of Roxanne's daughter, Lori, discovering the open closet in her bedroom, and then recording some mischievous children's voices. It was only to be a brief segment, but the crew had caught a severe case of the giggles. Every time they started to shoot the scene, a chain reaction of laughter spread everywhere. Even though we were sitting downstairs and couldn't see what was happening, such laughter is infectious and we cracked up every time we heard them blow another take. The things you learn about what goes on "behind the scenes"…

Then came time for the investigation. I had never conducted an investigation with this size TV crew before, and was doubtful as to how it could work with a couple of cameramen and a sound guy surrounding me and following my every move like a school of fish. But I have to say that they really knew what they were doing, and I was immediately put at ease. All I had to do was just focus on the investigation.

The other factor that really helped was that all the *Creepy Canada* guys were very nice and had great senses of humor—a crucial component to success in any endeavor! I quickly realized that this would not only be interesting, it would be fun!

I was hoping all the spirits would share my enthusiasm and also participate in the show…

The Creepy Canada crew zooms in on the EMF meter I'm holding, which is detecting high readings near the gates.

We started in the backyard, and as Lori snapped pictures, I scanned for EMF readings. There were actually some high readings in a couple of spots—well beyond what should normally exist, which would be little or nothing in an open yard with no sources of electricity. It was encouraging, but I was hoping for something a little more concrete. I would not be disappointed.

We all gathered inside the garage and closed the door. They were taping in infrared so it was quite dark, but there was still enough light to see where everyone was standing. At one point, I was in the southwest corner and could see that no one was within several feet of the long south wall. I followed the usual procedure and asked if anyone wanted to make their presence known by giving some sort of sign. Within moments there was a distinct "thud" several feet in front of me near the wall. Everyone heard it (more importantly the cameras recorded it), and from my line of vision I knew for certain it wasn't the result of any human action.

Moving forward, I carefully scanned the floor and found a package of rope that had somehow come off a nearby shelf. I picked it up and dropped it from the height of the shelf, and confirmed that was the same sound we had heard.

Here I am, in infrared, asking for a sign in the garage. Moments later the package of rope fell to the floor. (Clip from *Creepy Canada* episode.)

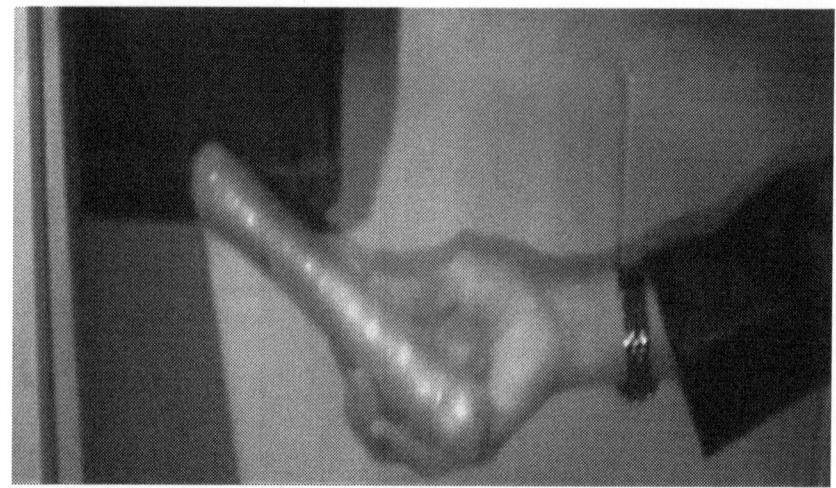

The package of rope. (Clip from *Creepy Canada* episode.)

Objects moving on command during a "live" ghost hunt! I was much too excited to be frightened. A little later there was another sound from the same area; this time it was a sharper, more metallic sound. I went over to look and found one of those clawed gardening tools on the floor, and I know it hadn't been there before. I also know that no one was anywhere near that shelf so it couldn't have been accidentally knocked onto the floor. Roxanne was able to confirm that both the rope and the tool were kept up on the shelf.

The tool that fell…or was pushed… (From *Creepy Canada* episode.)

Two objects moving! Could it get any better?

I was really into the investigation now, and all my senses were on high alert. I was fully expecting to hear or see something else fantastic, but I admit I wasn't quite prepared to *feel* something—something like a hand on my shoulder.

As there were often crew members to the left of me, and crew members to the right of me, I naturally assumed that when I felt one firm hand tap my right shoulder it was one of the crew members or Bob trying to get my attention and wanting me to turn around—which I immediately did, only to discover that no one was behind me!

I quickly turned left, and turned right, and accounted for every member of the crew, Bob, Roxanne and Lori, but none of these living participants had been within arms reach of me at the time.

"Did anyone just touch my shoulder?" I asked, controlled, but concerned.

Indeed, no one had been behind me, and no one had even been close enough at that moment to touch my shoulder. This was just too cool! Here I had been worried that nothing would happen with so many people around, and then I get rare physical contact! Maybe some people would have been terrified, but it wasn't threatening, and I was far more curious than scared.

Moments after I was tapped on the shoulder I ask if anyone had touched me in this manner. (Clip from *Creepy Canada* episode.)

Unfortunately, that was the end of the spooky phenomena in the garage for that night, but I couldn't consider the experience anything but an amazing success. There is always the fear that you're going to appear foolish carrying all this fancy equipment and then have absolutely nothing happen on national (or international) TV, but the active spirits of the Cemetery Gates house did not let us down. Skeptics may question the evidence, but I am one hundred percent confident of what I heard, saw and felt that night.

We wrapped up the investigation with the starting point for it all, the gates themselves. With the EMF meter I was able to trace a flow of energy that seemed to originate between the gates, where it was the strongest, then slowly dissipate the further up the driveway we went. It certainly appeared as though this was an energetic gateway to another world—a world that came from beyond and went straight into Roxanne's house and property.

It was truly a remarkable night. The only question that remained was how the *Creepy Canada* people would put it all together. I had never seen the show, so I had no clue what it would be like. There are some really terrible ghost shows out there, and I spent the next several months hoping this would not be one of them.

In the meantime, I proudly wore my *Creepy Canada* baseball cap throughout the winter. I often received puzzled looks, and occasionally someone had to ask, "What's creepy about Canada?" Invariably, after I explained, there was great interest in the show. Everyone loves a good ghost story!

Finally the following spring, I received notice that the DVDs of season three would soon be shipped. It was very nice of them to send the entire season, but of course I was most interested, and concerned, about the Cemetery Gates segment. When the package arrived, I tore it open as I hurried to the DVD player. I quickly scanned the episode list, found the Cemetery Gates episode, popped it in the player and held my breath. Would I be embarrassed? Would I hate it? Would I never live it down?

I breathed a sigh of relief just seconds into the show as I immediately saw that the *Creepy Canada* staff knew what they were doing. The opening frames clearly showed it was a quality production with great camerawork, and I was able to sit back and enjoy the show.

There were the scenes with Roxanne and Lori that flowed so smoothly on television, yet I knew what had gone on during the taping. There was the menacing phantom, who was really a nice guy. And there I was, the Ghost Investigator, thankfully not looking completely ridiculous—and believe me, Bob and my friends would have let me know if I had.

I was pleasantly surprised, and quite impressed, by the entire production. Here was what I look for in a ghost program—some background and eyewitness accounts of the haunting, depictions of actual events, and an attempt to gather evidence to support the paranormal phenomena. This was a ghost show that was actually entertaining—what a concept!

I let the DVD continue to run to the next segment, which I watched with great interest, and have continued to enjoy watching the other episodes of season three. Hopefully, there will be many more seasons to come.

While it's easy to get caught up in the whirl of a television show, the solemn fact still remains that uneasy spirits continue to dwell within these gates, making Roxanne and Lori's lives interesting, to say the least. I don't think I could live under such conditions, but they seem to have managed to learn to peacefully co-exist with entities that have not been able to rest in peace.

Will the gates continue to draw in lost souls like a paranormal magnet? That will most likely be the case, and we can only hope that the only menacing phantoms in the future are all actors…

Relaxing with my new Canadian friends after the show…

Alterations

Ellen and John moved into their Monroe, New York home in 2000. There had been two previous owners of the modest Cape Cod house built in 1952, and there hadn't been anything to indicate that they were buying more than they had bargained for.

However, a few months after moving in they began experiencing strange feelings in two particular locations. The closet in the second floor hallway was ordinary except for the fact that its sliding door never seemed to close properly. While that was a minor annoyance, it paled in comparison to the "bad feelings" it began to generate every time they passed by. And, as the closet was situated between their bedroom and the bathroom, they had to pass by it several times a day.

The other unpleasant location was the staircase leading from the kitchen down to the basement. While Ellen described the staircase as feeling uncomfortable to the point of seeming to be a place of darkness and the evil, her husband flat out "hated" that staircase and was always very reluctant to use it.

While nothing occurred that was overtly threatening, the "bad feelings" persisted and Ellen decided that something must be done. About this time she heard about the technique of smudging—an ancient practice using the smoke of burning herbs such as sage to clear the air of negative influences. She discussed this idea with her husband who thought it was worth trying, but before she was able to buy a sage smudge stick, an amazing thing happened.

Just a week after discussing the idea of smudging, John awoke in the middle of the night and for some reason felt compelled to go down into the basement. Descending the stairs he hated so much, he entered the basement and was startled by a man's voice speaking right next to him. No one was visible, but the voice was loud and clear, and it spoke in a completely normal and non-threatening tone. As unnerving as the ethereal voice was, however, what the phantom man said was even more remarkable.

"Please don't smudge us!" the disembodied voice implored.

Despite the understandable fear of the moment, John had the presence of mind to reply, "If you behave yourself we won't smudge you, but it you scare my wife we will."

At this point in the story, I believe it's important to pause and examine the implications of this incredible encounter. First of all, there is the extraordinary phenomenon of the manifested voice. Nowadays, so much is being made of garbled, indistinct EVP (electronic voice phenomena) recordings that it is refreshing to come upon a clear, genuine-sounding human voice that does not need to be computer enhanced or interpreted through the imagination of an optimistic ghost hunter.

The message itself is also remarkable in the choice of words this spirit used—he didn't say, "Please don't smudge *me*," he said, "Please don't smudge *us*." This, of course, implies that there are at least two spirits. This also implies that he is not only aware of this additional spirit or spirits, but he is also cognizant of what Ellen and John are talking about inside their home. Not very comforting to realize that ghosts are spying on you!

It is also intriguing to think that these ghosts do not want to be smudged, which suggests that the ancient practice would have some unpleasant or unwelcome effect upon them. Evidently they did not want to be disturbed or driven out of the house, and at least one of the ghosts was apparently irritated enough at the prospect that it decided to seek revenge.

Shortly after this incident, Ellen awoke around 2 or 3am to an overwhelming smell of cigarette smoke. It was so strong she said it was as if someone was standing over her blowing smoke right into her face. She actually gasped for air and choked on the thick cloud of smoke that seemingly engulfed her.

Neither she nor her husband smoked, and as it was winter and the windows were closed, the smoke could not be coming from outside. Although it clearly smelled like it was from a cigarette, Ellen knew this couldn't be possible, and became alarmed at the prospect that the house was on fire. Shaking her sleeping husband, she awakened him and asked, "Don't you smell that smoke?"

He didn't smell anything, and a thorough search of the house did not reveal anything burning. Was an angry spirit punishing Ellen for suggesting the smudging? Was this ghost somehow manifesting cigarette smoke and blowing it into her face as if to say, "See, how do you like it?"

Whether or not this was some type of paranormal retribution, the bizarre activity did not end that night. On at least six other occasions Ellen was awakened at the same time each night by the choking odor of cigarette smoke in her face. Unfortunately, she got little sympathy from John, who despite his encounter with the phantom voice, found the idea of a cigarette-smoking ghost hard to believe. Until it happened to him…

One night he woke up in the middle of the night, shook Ellen awake and asked, "What is this cigarette smoke in here!?"

On this particular occasion, Ellen couldn't smell a thing, and it appears that John was the sole target of the angry spirit that night. Perhaps that was some small payback for John initially agreeing to try the sage smoke to drive away the unwanted spirits. In any event, he immediately apologized to Ellen for not believing her before.

The cigarette smell never returned after that night. Perhaps once both of them had experienced it, the smoking spirit was satisfied that it had proven its point? While it was good that the annoying smoke stopped, that was not the end of all the activity.

In 2002, Ellen decided to leave her job and the weeks before her last day was a stressful time. They were also planning to undergo major renovations on the house, so the last thing she needed was anything else playing on her nerves—which is usually the perfect time for active spirits to play upon one's nerves…

Ellen was in the shower when she heard the phone ring. For some reason the ringing tone sounded different. It wasn't as loud as usual, but it was definitely a ringing phone and she wasn't about to get out of the shower to answer it. Whoever was calling could just leave a message.

The ringing stopped, and a moment later she could hear a very animated woman's voice going on and on. Ellen couldn't make out the words, just that it was a very happy sounding woman's voice leaving a very long message. Finally, after what seemed to take forever, the woman said what vaguely sounded like, "I love you. Bye!"

The voice was completely unfamiliar, and Ellen had no idea why anyone would be leaving such a long message, with such an affectionate ending. Not stopping to dry off, she grabbed a towel, wrapped it around herself and headed for the answering machine. She was stunned to find that the message light was not flashing. How could that be? Hitting the message play button anyway, the machine indicated that there were not any messages.

It was odd, but Ellen certainly didn't think it was a call from beyond. However, she started to get suspicious when the same thing happened the following week. Once again she was in the shower. The phone had that strange ring, and the same animated woman spoke for the same length of time, and ended her message with what sounded like an affectionate farewell. When Ellen checked the answering machine, there was no sign of a call. The machine was working perfectly, receiving other messages, but for some reason not from this woman.

Some contractors were coming to the house prior to the start of the renovations, and she asked a plumber to check to see if the phone line ran under the tub. Perhaps water was leaking, creating some kind of short circuit, or possibly picking up someone else's calls? The phone line wasn't near the tub, there weren't any leaks and no one could find anything wrong.

The plumber simply stated, "Just face it, you have a ghost!"

That was not what Ellen wanted to hear. She also didn't want to hear the strange noises that began in the basement a few days later.

This time, she didn't say anything to her husband about the phantom calls or noises in the basement. But it wasn't anything that would remain a secret, because John was experiencing his own talkative ghost.

He revealed to her that on two occasions when he was in the shower he heard a soft telephone ring, followed by a woman's voice. He stressed that this woman clearly had "the gift of gab," yet when he checked the answering machine there were no messages. Their experiences were identical, but who was this mysterious woman, why was she so happy, and to whom was she saying goodbye?

I suspect it was one of the female spirits in the house who knew she and the other trapped souls would soon be released, because the day that construction actually began, the haunting ceased. The terrible closet was removed, along with the staircase to the basement that also caused such discomfort. Whatever spiritual forces were locked into this location somehow were broken by the physical alterations of the structure. I have heard of many instances where haunting activity has begun during renovations, but there are also many cases where structural changes end the activity. And in this case, I think the ghosts knew what was about to happen, and were thankful for it!

Checking into the past of the house, the original owners were sisters. They had the house for many years, and there was just one other owner before Ellen and John. Further research into the lives of these people may shed some light on why spirits remained, but maybe in this case, the past should be left buried…

I contacted Ellen several months after the initial interview to arrange a visit to the house and take some pictures. I could detect some reluctance on her part, and she admitted that her husband didn't want me there in case I might "stir things up." Everything had been quiet, and John did not want to take any risks and possibly disturb their newfound peace.

Hey, I know when I'm not wanted!

But seriously, while I was somewhat disappointed, I certainly couldn't blame them for their decision. After all they had been though, the last thing I wanted to do was to take any chances of reactivating the trouble. There are plenty of other places I can go to start trouble…

Even though I never had the chance to personally investigate this haunting, I find it to be a fascinating case of conscious, interactive ghosts. I continue to hear "experts" declare that ghosts can't hurt you, and while no one was physically injured here, these ghosts knew how to push the buttons of the living and inflict psychological damage.

Hopefully, this will be the last I hear of this case, and barring any further alterations—structural or spiritual—the living will go on living happily, and the dead will rest in peace.

The Evil That Men Do

In February of 2005 when Jenny went to view the 1960s contemporary style house in Pomona, New York, she noticed a memorial plaque hanging in the living room, but she didn't pay much attention to it. Perhaps she should have looked a little closer at the names of the two deceased people, because although the plaque was gone when she moved in, the dead would still insist on being remembered.

The house had been on the market for over a year, which was unusual considering the sizzling real estate market throughout Rockland County. However, there was no time to wonder about that after signing the lease agreement, as in addition to all the unpacking, the place needed a thorough cleaning. Things were finally falling into place after about three weeks, but unfortunately, that was when everything else began falling apart—literally!

One evening when Jenny and her fiancé were cleaning on the first floor, they heard a crashing sound upstairs. They discovered that a glass shelf in the bathroom had smashed on the floor, but it wasn't a simple accident. The shelf had been firmly attached to the wall by brackets, and Jenny had put three candles on it. To their amazement, they found that the candles were now standing neatly along the edge of the sink, which was six feet away, so they had to be carried and placed there before the shelf came off the wall.

The broken shelf also presented a puzzle, as it did not fall straight down. It was under the sink, also six feet away from where it had been mounted on the other side of the room. Though shattered in many pieces, the rectangular shape was intact and there wasn't even the smallest piece of broken glass anywhere else onthe floor.

Quite an unsettling mystery! Somehow three candles were moved from the shelf, transported across the room and set down on the sink. The glass shelf was then lifted up off its brackets, carried across the room and smashed on the floor under the sink. It had clearly not been a natural occurrence, but what unnatural force had done this, and why?

On a mirror above the sink, a little girl had scratched her name into the glass. Was this her way of letting the new residents know she was still there? This girl's name is also carved into the woodwork of

13

the spiral staircase that stretches from the basement to the second floor. This staircase has also been the center of much of the unusual activity in the house. A coincidence, or further evidence that the dead were not pleased with the new tenants?

One evening Jenny was standing on the stairs and her little dog was sitting a few steps below her. Her fiancé was standing on the first floor speaking to her, and they both watched in amazement as the dog was suddenly shoved backwards off the step by some unseen force. This spiral staircase is made of metal and wood, and it's lucky the poor dog wasn't seriously hurt as it plummeted downward and landed hard one flight below.

Unfortunately, the dog's luck would soon run out. Although the dog never wanted to go out after dark, late one night he insisted on being let out. He also never went far from the house, but this night he went all the way down the long driveway into the street and was hit by a passing car. He was killed instantly.

Still devastated by the loss a few months later, Jenny decided to get a new puppy. The litter of puppies she went to see had all been checked out by the vet and had been certified healthy. However, soon after bringing her new friend home he started to act sick. He was diagnosed as having the parvovirus, and after several days at the vet the poor little puppy died. Inexplicably, the rest of the litter remained healthy, even though the virus is highly contagious. Jenny was beginning to feel that something in that house didn't like dogs.

One woman who visited the house claimed to have psychic abilities. She felt that there were three spirits there, and at least one was hostile to animals. She believed that the first dog had been lured out to the road to his death. I seriously hope this is not the case, because any spirit that would hurt a dog needs to have its spiritual butt exorcised right out of this plane of existence.

Despite this warning, and the death of two dogs in just a few months, Jenny still wanted a canine companion. This time she chose a big strong dog. However, even he fell ill his first two weeks in the house, but fortunately he recovered and has been doing fine ever since.

He is usually a very happy, active dog. However, there is a mirror in the bedroom where he often seems to catch sight of something near the dresser, and begins to growl in a menacing manner. Otherwise, he doesn't pay much attention to the strange activity in the house.

The spiral staircase was also the site of one of the most pronounced paranormal events in the house. Jenny, her father, and her friend, Vicky, were sitting in the living room one evening. They were complaining about the ghost when they suddenly heard loud, heavy footsteps descending from the second floor. At least eight feet of the staircase is completely open and exposed to view from the living room, and the three listened in astonishment as the footsteps pounded their way down the wooden steps to the level of the living room floor—but no one was visible!

Then, just as quickly, the phantom footsteps hurried back up the staircase to the second floor. They waited breathlessly to see what would happen next, but there was only silence. Their complaints about the ghost had clearly provoked a tantrum, but fortunately this time no one got hurt.

On at least six other occasions Jenny has fallen down a flight of stairs. They are not the safest of stairs, but each time she felt as though she had been shoved from behind. While dangerous episodes such as this were all the convincing Jenny needed of a haunting, her fiancé needed a more convincing example. And he got it. Big time.

He awoke one night to see a dark silhouette of a man just a few feet away, standing between the bed and the dresser (the area where the dog stares and growls). The figure of the man just seemed to be watching him for a few moments, then vanished. Her fiancé quickly turned on the light, and was not ashamed to admit that he kept the light on the rest of that sleepless night! Later that same night, the faucet in the adjoining bathroom turned itself on, as if anyone needed further proof of the paranormal resident.

Jenny realized she needed some answers. One day when the caretaker was doing some work on the property she asked if he knew of any strange activity in the house. He asked what she meant, and without going into details, she explained that odd things were going on.

"I wouldn't doubt it!" the caretaker declared, and then added with great conviction, "That house needs to be burned down!"

A stunning statement! What secrets does this man know about this place, and why did he feel that the best thing to do was burn the house to the ground? Jenny wanted to know more, but all the caretaker would say was that a Jewish man had died in the house a few years earlier. He did not elaborate on the circumstances of the death, or the nature and character of the deceased. I would be willing, however, to place a small wager that the man hadn't been fond of dogs!

There have been many other strange happenings in this house, both day and night. The television turns itself on, doors open and close, one particular wine stopper always comes out of its rack, there are voices (usually of little girls), noises of all kinds, and classic cold spots. Sometimes when it all gets too much for Jenny she yells, "Not today, I'm too busy to deal with this!" That sometimes works, for a short time.

Vicky has witnessed many instances of these bizarre events, and after reading one of my *Ghost Investigator* books, she convinced Jenny to contact me with her story. I have to say that the ensuing email was one of the most comprehensive and concise lists of experiences I've ever received. A couple of weeks later I was on my way to this unique Pomona house.

It certainly didn't appear to be the kind of house one typically associates with a haunting. Set on a large wooded piece of property, the builders seem to have been trying to convey a modern look, with rustic overtones. In other words, it's one of those many Rockland houses built in the 1960s and '70s that doesn't quite fit the suburban landscape. It was well constructed, though, and there are plenty of large windows to let in the light and enjoy the view of the trees surrounding the house.

The most unsettling part of the structure is the three-story spiral staircase, which was placed in the center of the house where it doesn't benefit from much natural light. Its open design, tight turning radius, and cold, hard materials do not make for an inviting main passageway through the house. It just does not provide a sense of security whether ascending or descending. Of course, ghostly footsteps, and being shoved in the back don't exactly give one a soft and fuzzy feeling here, either.

Jenny and Vicky gave me a quick tour of the house so I could get my bearings. As I climbed the stairs for the first time, I wondered that Jenny only fell down half a dozen times. There were a few fleeting EMF readings, but other than that, and a general feeling of uneasiness, nothing happened on that staircase during my time there.

The main bedroom was another story. For some inexplicable reason, there were high EMF readings just along the right side of the bed. This is the side of the bed where her fiancé sleeps, the side where he saw the dark figure standing and where the dog growls at something. Jenny and Vicky suggested I see if the clock radio on Jenny's side of the bed could be the source of the EMF. While there was a high reading directly in front of the display, the field quickly diminished and the left side of the bed was at zero. It simply was not possible for the clock radio to be the source of the electromagnetic field on the opposite side of the bed.

After taking more readings, I was able to confirm that whatever strange energy was present, it was only detectable on the right side of the bed, from the pillow down to near the foot of the bed—essentially the exact area where a person would be stretched out. I was reminded of the case of the Peach Grove Inn in Warwick, NY, (*Ghost Investigator, Volume 1*) where a phantom dog is seen (and felt) jumping up onto the end of a bed. Just the foot of that bed had high EMF readings, like some paranormal residue or perhaps the signpost of a spot where spirits enter our world and conduct their haunting.

Jenny then told me of another fascinating, and terrifying, story involving that bedroom and the right side of the bed. It was about 4am, and she was in bed waiting for her fiancé to come home. There was no question of her being wide awake, as she had just made a phone call. This is her description of the incident in her own words:

"I thought my fiancé pulled into the driveway. I heard the gravel on the driveway, heard the front door open and close, heard heavy footsteps up the stairs, heard the bedroom door open and close, heard someone walking into the bedroom, then felt someone sit on the bed beside me. I pretended to be asleep the entire time, but when I didn't feel any more movement after a few seconds I rolled over to see what was going on. I noticed an indentation in the bed, but no one was there!"

Someone came home and went to bed that night, just no one alive…

We then went to a room on the other side of the house. It isn't used as a bedroom or an office. In fact, its only use is spiritual, as religious items fill two tables and candles devoted to various saints burn in an effort to bring some level of protection to the house. There is a different feeling here, a sort of calmness as if a benevolent spiritual shield or buffer guards the occupants of this room from the more hostile forces holding sway over the rest of the house. This was reminiscent of the house in Summit, New Jersey—known as the Most Haunted House in New Jersey (see *GI V1*)—where opposing positive and negative forces appear to have split the house down the middle.

There was just one fleeting EMF reading in that "safe room," as if something lingered just long enough to make its presence known and then moved on. The event was duly noted.

I did poke my head, and camera, into the attic. It can only be reached from a panel in the ceiling of the closet, and it's all just rafters and insulation—and more dust than you could imagine. I didn't go all the way up for several reasons. There wasn't a floor to walk on and the space was so confining I wouldn't have been able to stand up. Crawling across filthy rafters was not appealing, and if I slipped and stuck a leg through the sheetrock, Jenny would have lot of explaining to do to the landlord. (Although I think it's the landlord who has some explaining to do about this place!)

Also, I was fighting a nasty upper respiratory infection, and forty-year-old dust and insulation—and god knows what else—would not have been welcome additions to my lungs.

Still, I had to take a look up in the attic, because Jenny told me that on several occasions they have heard a man's heavy footsteps pacing back and forth up there. With the thick blanket of insulation (and did I mention all that dust?), it would be impossible for anything natural to make the sounds of footsteps in that attic. When I climbed down off the ladder, Jenny and Vicky were kind enough to pull the dust bunnies (dust rhinos would be more accurate) from my hair. I shook and wiped myself down, and proceeded with the investigation.

The bathroom was very interesting, but not due to any evidence I found that night. Whenever someone tries to explain an unusual event, I try to picture the surroundings and circumstances, but as the saying goes, there's nothing like being there. While I could imagine the glass shelf and the candles, actually seeing the room where the event occurred made the entire scenario gel.

The shelf brackets were sturdy and secure. The sink was six feet away from where the shelf had been mounted. It was immediately obvious that there would have been absolutely no way the candles could have fallen off the shelf and all landed upright and in a line on the edge of the sink, after having traveled six feet through the air. I also could not envision any way in which the shelf could accidentally have lifted off the brackets, hit the floor, but not have broken until it traveled six feet across the room and only then shattered to pieces under the sink. I would defy any skeptic to explain this one.

We then decided to sit quietly in the hall by the staircase for a while. I began with my usual questions, asking if anyone wanted to give us a sign, then remaining silent for a minute to see if anything happened. Just after I asked, the lights in Jenny's bedroom flickered. Interesting, but not necessarily supernatural. Then I asked if someone had a message to communicate to us. Just seconds later there was a deep pounding sound that seemed to come from the basement and resonated throughout the house.

I was definitely leaning toward the supernatural for this one, but first I had to ask if it could be the dog. Jenny told me he was outside. Again, the powerful, resonant pounding rose up from the basement, just after I asked if anything was in the basement. The tension was increasing with every sound.

I then asked if there was someone there who had died in the house. Instantly, a loud thud and menacing whirring sound shook the house, and it hadn't come from the basement, it was directly beneath us on the first floor. My eyes probably were close to popping out of my head as I considered the possibility that some angry spirit was crashing and banging his way up from the basement, directly toward us. Then Jenny quickly informed me that the jarring sound was just from the refrigerator, and that it did that all the time. We had a good laugh over it, and it seemed to clear the tension from the air—for the moment.

Moving into the bedroom, I set up the infrared camcorder and prepared to wait to see if anything happened. We didn't have to wait long. Within a minute there was another deep sound that Vicky aptly described as a "rumbling." It continued on and off for a brief time and I finally categorized it as some "serious banging." I asked if anything in the bedroom wanted to give a sign, but again there was a sound beneath us toward the back of the house (the dog was in the front yard, so we could once again rule out him as the source of the noise). We all agreed that it seemed as though something was beckoning us to the basement.

Generally, in the ghost hunting field if something beckons, you follow. Even if you don't like it.

Vicky volunteered to go outside with the dog, just to assure that he didn't scratch on the door or make any sound we might misinterpret. Jenny and I went into the basement and stood near the washing machine, which had once turned itself on. The washing machine stood next to a large pile of furniture and boxes from several previous owners. Perhaps some of this phantom man's earthly property is still stored in this area, as it's the only section of the basement that seems to have any unusual activity.

We waited silently in the dark, bracing ourselves for the loud pounding we had heard earlier. But there was nothing, only silence. Somewhat nervous anticipation turned to slight irritation. I spoke out and said that if there was something here that had the power to make a banging sound, couldn't it at least tap on something now? Long seconds passed, then there was a noise, but not in the basement where we stood. Now the sound—which Jenny described as a "thunk"—came from high above us, probably from the second floor. There were more to follow.

So, I thought, we were on the second floor and the sounds came from the basement. We go down to the basement and the sounds start on the second floor. We were being played—an old spirit trick I have unfortunately been a party to several times.

"Are you playing games with us?" I asked.

Several loud taps responded from high above us.

"I guess they want us back upstairs," Jenny commented and then said, "Maybe we can hear them better in the chute."

I wondered what she was talking about, then she pointed out a shaft that ran from the basement to the second floor. It was a laundry chute, and the opening must have helped sound travel throughout the house. Just another odd feature of this place...

We went up to the first floor, and while I perched on the end of a bench in the living room, Jenny checked the stairs for EMF readings. There were several high readings directly on the steps again. Then there was an odd sound, this time seeming to come from the room we were in—which was something new that night.

"What was that?" I asked.

"I don't know," Jenny responded.

I said that I thought it sounded like a voice, but it wasn't speaking words. I described it as something like a "whoop," and Jenny agreed "that was exactly" what she heard, too. And since we were the only two people in the house, we had no way to explain this one.

We waited, and asked for more signs. Seconds ticked by in silence. My concentration was broken for a few moments as my camcorder stopped because the DVD was full. I weighed the pros and cons of waiting for the disk to format. (The DVD media Sony included with the camcorder needed about five minutes to format before it could be removed. You would think with all the money you spend on one of

The infamous laundry chute.

their high-end camcorders, they could spend a few cents and give you a better DVD.) I decided to just run with the digital audio recorder—a decision I would come to regret.

Just after I turned off the camcorder, there was another sound in the large open living room. This time it was a rasping, almost grinding type of sound, as if someone was trying to clear his throat, or was trying to speak in one of those very guttural languages that always reminds me of someone about to spit. In another words, it wasn't the most appealing sound, but it was clear and distinct, and Jenny said she had never heard anything like it before in the house.

Shortly after, Vicky came back inside with the dog. He was still very excited that a visitor was there, and he ran around with boundless energy. Just as I thought that his activity would preclude gathering anymore evidence, a shadow passed across the curtains at the front of the living room.

Let me set the scene: The room is a large rectangle, and I was sitting in the southwest corner. Vicky and Jenny were sitting in the northwest corner. The east wall is composed of very tall windows, which continue on along half of the north wall. Curtains covered the windows, but a light outside was able to permeate the material and create a soft glow the length of the windows.

I was diagonally across from the corner of those windows, and saw a shadow pass quickly from right to left. I assumed that the light must be from a bright streetlight on the road, and that perhaps a large truck had just driven by and momentarily obscured the light. A reasonable explanation, right? Too bad I was completely wrong.

My scenario would only work if the light was at a distance, and some object passing between the light and the house blocked a discreet portion of it as it moved from right to left. The light, in fact, was mounted directly on the corner of the house outside of the windows. I was stunned. Obviously, a truck was out of the question! But even if a bat or some other creature had passed in front of the light, on the inside it would have appeared as though the entire light blinked off and then on. This was definitely not the case and I quickly realized that given the angle and position of the light, and the large shadow I witnessed moving from right to left, only one explanation fit these circumstances—whatever blocked the light had been *inside* of the living room!

The object had to be solid and roughly between five and six feet high, and a foot or so wide, and it had to pass *in front* of the curtains in order to block the light in the manner I observed. It also had to be capable of moving swiftly along the two walls without being impeded by the furniture. Quite a trick! While I am absolutely certain what I saw, I am not quite so sure what it was, although I certainly have my suspicions, of the paranormal variety. Perhaps this was a glimpse of the man who had died in the house, who continues to make his footsteps heard, who has appeared in the bedroom, and who doesn't care for dogs. It was at this point that I regretted not having the camcorder running.

But all was not lost, as I shall explain shortly.

We tried to continue to record audio while sitting quietly, but the dog could no longer contain his enthusiasm. He excitedly beat his tail on the floor, barked, and basically insisted upon the attention he deserved after being a good dog all evening. It was fine with me as I wasn't feeling that great and was content to pack up and go home with all the photos, video and audio I had collected.

Over the next week or so, I felt a lot worse before I started feeling better, so it was a while before I reviewed all the evidence. I was not surprised that the various banging noises we heard in the basement (when he were on the second floor), as well as the banging and tapping sounds we heard on the second floor (when we were in the basement), could not clearly be heard on the audio recording. The bizarre sounds in the living room were more distinct. I didn't see anything out of the ordinary on the camcorder footage, either in normal light or in infrared.

As I started to carefully go over each photo, I began to despair that I hadn't obtained any additional evidence. Photo after photo appeared on my computer screen, as I thought, *Nothing, nothing, nothing. What the…?*

On one of the last photos, which had been taken of the living room windows, I saw a dark area that looked unusual. The photo had been taken in infrared and was very dark overall, but something was clearly blocking the light coming through the curtains. Where had I seen that before!

I lightened and enlarged the photo incrementally, and with each step I could see a dark figure begin to take on a more defined shape. Someone, or something, had been standing in front of the window!

My heart beat a little faster as I tried to render some detail out of the mysterious figure. However, no matter what I tried I could only get a solid black shape silhouetted in front of the dimly lit curtains. I was very excited, but still cautious. The last thing I wanted to do was run around proclaiming I had photographed a ghost and then find out there was a perfectly natural explanation.

I emailed the photo to Jenny and asked if she had any rational explanation. I personally didn't recall her being in any of the living room pictures, but I needed to know if she remembered being in front of the window when I was taking the photographs. Her response was that she remembered that she and Vicky made a point of making sure they were out of the way whenever I was taking a picture.

When I went over the audio again, I made note of when I took that photo, as the sound of the digital camera was unmistakable. It had been when Vicky was outside with the dog, which ruled her out. And I have to admit to being pleased to discover that at the moment I snapped that picture, Jenny was by the staircase—at least 25 feet away from that window!

Still cautious, I emailed the image to Mike Worden for his expert opinion. He felt that the figure was definitely in the room, and was curious as to why there wasn't the slightest hint of any lighter sections or shading on the figure. Playing the devil's advocate and supposing that it actually was Jenny in the photo, he asked if she had been dressed all in black. It was an excellent point! I recalled that she was wearing a black skirt and a white blouse. White always shows up well in infrared, yet this figure was solid black from top to bottom.

This was one astonishing image, and something I had been waiting years to photograph. I think I can finally say with some certainty that I have a picture of a ghost!

The remarkable dark figure. I had to brighten the original image so it would show up in print. Upon further research, I determined that the figure was approximately five feet, eight inches tall.

The living room in daylight. Note that there isn't anything in the room that could have caused that dark figure.

Naturally, I was anxious to get back to this house for another investigation. I knew the clock was ticking, as Jenny would be moving out during the summer. It was clear that there were many layers of activity here—some benign, some helpful and at least one hostile. And no pun intended, but that photo of the dark figure haunted me. If a spirit was strong enough to manifest a solid figure right in front of me, I needed to know more about this menacing, dark entity.

I had been impressed by a local psychic, Lisa Ann, when I met her at the house in Monroe where the little boy has an "imaginary" friend, and claims that his friend died on the property and his body is buried in the basement (see *GI V5*). Without any prior knowledge of the place or the situation, Lisa Ann sensed the presence of this boy's spirit (among several others at this very haunted location) and even felt that there may indeed be bones under the house. This was the type of insight and ability I needed at the Pomona house.

However, the investigation would turn out to be the easy part—getting a day that agreed with the schedules of Jenny, Lisa Ann and myself would prove to be nearly impossible. Fortunately, with a mere twelve days left before moving day, it all clicked. As Lisa Ann and I drove to the house we talked about all kinds of things, except the Pomona haunting. I made sure I didn't even bring up the subject, so there wasn't any chance of slipping and revealing any details. I needed to be certain that I did not influence her in any way, and had informed Jenny not to say anything about what had been occurring until Lisa Ann had a chance to go through the house and say what she had found.

On the way home, it was interesting to hear Lisa Ann say that she thought I was bringing her somewhere that had a few things that went bump in the night, with perhaps a mild-mannered ghost or two. That preconception was crushed under the oppressive atmosphere of the place as soon as we pulled into the driveway. Within seconds she knew this was not going to be pleasant.

Jenny and I remained silent while Lisa Ann walked around the house, quickly scribbling notes on what she was "seeing." When she was ready to speak, I have to admit that I was startled by the nature of the strong and persistent impressions she received. Her initial impression was that the primary haunting is from a man, who appears as a dark figure in the bedroom (Jenny's fiancée did see him there) and other places around the house. Everywhere she had the sense that this had been some kind of doctor's office, but she repeatedly felt something was wrong every time she thought "doctor."

A few moments passed as her impressions were refined, and she realized this man was not a real doctor, but that he liked to conduct medical experiments, and was something of a psychopath. The term "butcher" was more appropriate to what she was sensing about this evil spirit.

As if that wasn't disturbing enough, she saw that there were many children connected to this place, but not in a happy way. In addition to the bizarre tests and procedures this man conducted on unsuspecting women, Lisa Ann had the "overwhelming feeling" that he also performed illegal abortions that may have led to the death of at least one adolescent girl.

With this, Jenny gasped. Just two nights earlier there had been a new phenomenon—a baby, or little girl, screaming for help. It was in the evening, she was upstairs, and an instant after she heard the scream she ran downstairs to see if something had possibly happened to her dog, and she had misinterpreted a canine yelp for a human child's cry. She found her fiancée and the dog in the living room, both calm and undisturbed. There hadn't been any strange sounds, let alone screaming, her fiancé said, but Jenny knew what she heard. And now with what Lisa Ann just said, it seemed to be an affirmation that there were some spirits of children also trapped in this house.

To make matters worse, if that was possible at this point, Lisa Ann believed this pseudo-doctor delighted in "pushing people's buttons," trying to see how far he could drive them until they broke. He victimized people in this manner when he was alive, and was still up to his old tricks even after death. Jenny had definitely rented the wrong house!

There were several areas of concentrated energy. The most potent was the spiral staircase—where the majority of the activity in the house has actually occurred. Lisa Ann felt that many spirits came and went through this column of energy that stretched from the basement to the top floor. She described being on those stairs as like being in another world, and I could also attest to the disorienting and unpleasant feelings there.

Another intense location was the small front bedroom. This place seemed to be a focal point for the horrors that occurred in the house, and it was here that Lisa Ann experienced the "sickest" feeling. She kept seeing "all kinds of medical stuff" in that room, women who were sick and scared, and blood everywhere.

The large room at the north end of the basement reminded Lisa Ann of something like a morgue, or at least a storage area for "many specimens in jars," as well as "body parts in a refrigerator." She repeated the idea of rows of jars lining shelves in this room, and Jenny recalled what she had found when she first moved in. She had indeed found a couple of jars in a section of the basement, and for some reason she "was afraid to touch them" so left them there. We looked at them, but they didn't appear to contain anything suspicious—which doesn't mean they never did.

Throughout the house, Lisa Ann kept seeing this sadistic man lurking in corners, trying to frighten her. She described him as a short man with a slight build, and a moustache that appeared old-fashioned. He didn't like being seen, and became even angrier when his tactics failed to scare her.

I asked if this hostility could have been directed at the two dogs that had died, and she believed it was possible, as dogs have a sixth sense and would have been able to see him. There was certainly hostility in the air throughout the house, and an uncomfortable pressure that manifested itself in me as a headache. Both Jenny and Lisa Ann also said they had headaches that began as soon as we began the investigation.

The next interesting revelation was when Lisa Ann declared that there is so much negativity in the walls of this house that the only way it is ever going to be cleared is if "it is torn down." As the caretaker had also stated that this place should be burned down, I saw that a majority opinion was forming! Lisa Ann went on to say that she almost never says such a thing, that it contradicts her belief system that if you don't want spirits you simply ask them to leave. But this innocuous looking house in Pomona appears to be too steeped in evil to be left standing.

However, not every entity here is negative. On my first visit, I felt a calm presence in the room where Jenny burns candles among the religious statues and pictures. Lisa Ann also felt this presence, and believes it is an older woman who is very protective. Perhaps she is somehow trying to prevent the evil man from victimizing any more women. Then, of course, there are the children—most definitely plural.

There might also be a young woman who died on the staircase. This was something Jenny and her friend had learned while using a pendulum, in much the manner of an Ouija board. Lisa Ann thought that a woman may have fallen to her death on those steps, possibly in an attempt to escape from the "butcher."

We continued moving from room to room and floor to floor, following the psychic trail of clues. Each time we descended the staircase to the basement, Lisa Ann saw the man standing in the doorway by the laundry chute. I asked if he was trying to prevent us from entering the laundry room, or was he trying to draw our attention to something. She thought for a moment, and felt that he stood there because there was something in the chute to which he was connected, some kind of evidence as to who he had been.

We examined the basement section of the chute and Lisa Ann found an old Rheingold beer can from the 1960s wedged behind one of the boards in the frame. Jenny had never noticed it before, and while a beer can did not support any of the theories as to what had transpired in this house, it was interesting to immediately find something from the timeframe in which these terrible events may have occurred.

We went back upstairs where a determined Lisa Ann bent over, head first, into the chute to search for more clues. While this was not a typical position for a psychic to assume during a ghost investigation, I applauded her efforts to go the extra mile—as we both quietly hoped she didn't go the extra two floors down to the basement!

As Lisa Ann hung mostly upside down in the chute, Jenny and I discussed the man who built the house. We did not know if he fit the physical description of the man Lisa Ann kept seeing, and we didn't know his profession. All we knew was that he died from cancer in the house. The caretaker had also mentioned that he thought that the original owner was Jewish. Just as we were wondering if that was the case, Lisa Ann's fingertips brushed against something stuck between pieces of wood in the dark chute. She didn't know what is was, but was amazed when she pulled out a matchbook for a Kosher deli in Spring Valley, NY. Again, this was not definitive proof, but the timing was remarkable. Just as Jenny and I were pondering if the man in question was Jewish, Lisa Ann found the matchbook.

A few moments later she pulled out a more disturbing find—a pair of little girl's frilly

The dusty matchbook Lisa Ann found in the laundry chute.

socks, that had collected decades of dust. There was nothing scary about them per se, but given all of the events that may have taken place, and the possibility of the spirits of children being present, the small, fancy socks made us all feel a bit queasy.

So, there were girl's socks, a Jewish deli matchbook and an old beer can—hardly proof of a haunting, or of unsavory medical practices taking place, yet tantalizing pieces in a bizarre puzzle.

Jenny called the caretaker, who was nice enough to take the time to stop by. We asked what the original owner had looked like, and he described him as being short, with a slight build, and he often wore facial hair in different styles. That certainly fit Lisa Ann's description. However, instead of being a man in the medical profession, the caretaker said that the original owner had been in the clothing business. Of course, who can tell what someone does in his spare time, behind the closed doors of his own home? And there had been other residents, so there are other potential candidates.

We do have some names to research, and hopefully neighbors and acquaintances will someday come forward with more information. For now, there is a more pressing concern. As relieved as I was that Jenny was moving out, I was quite disturbed to hear that a family was moving in—a family with a single child, a young girl. If the evil man decides to continue tormenting occupants, then he will be getting a prime target.

We all discussed what, if anything, we could do about it. Lisa Ann and Jenny suggested "accidentally" leaving one of my books and business cards behind on a shelf or in a closet. However, the more I thought about it, the less inclined I was to plant that seed in the new occupants. There is always a chance they may not be bothered. Although, admittedly, my confidence level in that regard is low, so I gave the caretaker my phone number. In the unfortunate event that things begin to happen to this girl or her parents, he will tell them about me and we'll see if we can do something to end this haunting.

Even though months have passed, I can still vividly recall seeing that dark shape pass before the curtains, and I am still amazed by the photograph with the mysterious figure. It is probably the best ghost photo I have taken in my career, and I have showed it to many other ghost hunters and they agree it's the "real deal."

As thrilling as this photo is, however, in a case such as this it's not easy to be pleased about any aspect of it. An evil man who may have experimented on young girls, who still torments the living and kills dogs is not something that should exist on this plane. Perhaps knowledge and awareness will stop him, or perhaps it will take some heavy duty spiritual force to oppose him.

Let us not forget the children, too, who may still be victims even in spirit, as well as the gentle woman who is trying to protect the innocent.

In the end, such persistent evil may require that this house in Pomona be knocked down and burned. But even then, could anyone guarantee that the next house built on this site wouldn't become inhabited by this entity?

Unfortunately, there are no guarantees in life, and certainly no guarantees in death. Shakespeare was correct when he wrote that, "The evil that men do lives after them," but hopefully some day even this evil will die.

Ghost Hunting Merit Badge

The best way to conduct a ghost hunt is in a quiet and controlled manner. Neither of these terms is likely to apply to a large group of adolescent girls in a haunted house. However, there is strong evidence to suggest that young girls are very sensitive to ghostly activity, and their considerable energy may actually assist in manifesting spirit energy. So it was with great curiosity and mixed expectations that I accepted an invitation to conduct a ghost hunt with some local Girl Scouts on the chilly and rainy night of December 29, 2005.

The site itself was irresistible—a historic house and former stagecoach stop, known as McGarrah's Inn, that was built in the 1790s in Monroe, New York. It also happens to contain the oldest Masonic Lodge in the state (and the third oldest in the country). I was told it was reputedly haunted, but in this case I didn't want to know all the details before the investigation. I would let the evidence, if any, speak for itself.

McGarrah's Inn in Monroe, NY, as it may have looked centuries ago. (I digitally removed the street signs, telephone poles and electrical lines.)

All in all, it was a unique opportunity, made possible by the Cornerstone Masonic Historical Society's president, Claude Horstmann. The fact that the old building is even still standing is also the result of Claude's foresight and determination to preserve the historic structure. When a local car dealer was eyeing the property, Claude fought to raise both awareness and the finances to keep the beautiful two-centuries-old house from the wrecking ball. His goal was to preserve the place as a museum of the area's history, as well as restoring it to a functioning lodge for the Masons.

When I arrived, my first impression was that this was one of the most stately looking houses in the area—a real colonial gem which I would love to be able to call home. However, as I grabbed my bags of equipment and headed inside, I had to remind myself that many old homes come with a steep price, one that is above and several steps beyond the financial commitment. Old homes can have very old inhabitants, and I have no desire to co-habitate with ghosts, friendly or not. A haunted house is a great place to visit, but I wouldn't want to live in one!

A group of about two dozen Girl Scouts, parents, a couple of boys, and Claude and his wife, Marilyn, soon gathered at several long tables in an open room by the back entrance. After a brief introduction and orientation, we got underway with what was easily the largest and most eager collection of junior ghost hunters I had ever encountered. While there would be some screaming in the next few hours, I have to say right off that this was one brave group of Girl Scouts, ready and willing to face the unknown in the darkness of this mysterious old house. I don't know if I would have had the courage to do something like this at their age.

I quickly discovered that simply trying to maneuver through the crowd with all of the equipment was going to be a challenge. Fortunately, I was able to hand over the camcorder to the capable hands of John Marks, and a couple of the Scouts volunteered to hold the tape recorder.

The first unusual thing I found was an area of high EMF readings at the base of the staircase by the doorway to the front parlor. Some of the girls suddenly felt cold, and most reported an uncomfortable feeling. Requesting that everyone remain silent, I asked if there was anything there that wanted to give us a sign of its presence. As if on cue, the infrared camcorder captured a few white spots moving through the air, but they could have simply been specks of dust. The high EMF readings then disappeared along with the chill in the air, and I became somewhat encouraged that there would be some measurable paranormal activity that night.

The scene from the main staircase. Present that night were: Lauren Reece, Kayla Marks, Amanda Marks, Ava Hegarty, Brianna Kousin, Francesca Verendia, Caila Friedman, Tommy Friedman, Rebecca Vitelli, Christy Somers, Jessica Simmons, Jessica Metellus, Kristen Mitchell, Danielle Guarneri, Sharon Murray, Christine Patrissi, Nicholas Mitchell, Lauren Murray, Lee Friedman, John Marks, Lynette Marks and Barbara Vitelli. The Girl Scouts were from Monroe Troops 524, 489 and 163.

When we moved into the parlor, there was a palpable mass of cold air near the doorway, extending over the couch, along with an odd sensation that something else was in the room with us. The temperature was 64 degrees in that area, but suddenly rose to 75 degrees, and the odd feeling dissipated. The introduction of so many warm bodies into the room might account for the increase in temperature, but I had the sense that this was an area of interest. Claude later confirmed that witnesses had seen a figure near the doorway and base of the staircase, and that the staircase itself has been the center of a lot of unusual activity. Marilyn later told me that during our investigation she heard footsteps on that staircase when the rest of us were in another part of the house.

The next stop was a small bathroom that the girls who had been here before all agreed was "creepy." Unfortunately, I wasn't able to obtain any creepy readings or photos to substantiate the claims in that room, but directly across the hall was a little storeroom that gave me a few surprises. As I stepped inside, my EMF meter started to rise, and I started to fall! There was something slick and slimy on the floor and I regained my balance just in time to prevent some very expensive equipment, and my bones, from hitting the floor.

Naturally, my author's mind envisioned all manner of gruesome substances, but the reality turned out to be quite mundane—a liquid soap container was leaking. As I carefully slid my feet across the floor of the small room, the EMF meter went up and registered over two. Despite a mass of Girl Scouts blocking the doorway, a chill swept into the room and I was suddenly covered in goose bumps. Then there was a creaking sound; not in the floor beneath me, but in the ceiling above me. It sounded just like someone walking on the floor above the storeroom. However, there wasn't anyone on the second floor, so the footsteps were not coming from a living being.

The EMF meter suddenly returned to zero and the sounds and chill ceased. I waited a few moments, and then with several Scouts looking on, I asked if whatever was present had the power to make the meter go up again. Right on cue the temperature dropped and the meter went up! I was pleasantly surprised by the response and was able to repeat the request and subsequent response several times with many witnesses. It was an impressive display of a conscious entity wishing to make its presence known to us!

At this point, the crowd of girls was pressing toward the doorway, as everyone wanted to experience the sensations in that room. Like trying to exit a subway train at rush hour, I squeezed my way out, went into the kitchen and waited while each girl had her chance to experience a taste of the paranormal.

The kitchen itself didn't appear to have any activity, but the back staircase leading up to the next floor had been the location of several sightings. A little boy has been seen on those stairs—at times when no children were in the house.

An infrared image looking up the main stairwell to the second and third floors.

Our large group then made our way up to the second floor, via the main staircase where I had first gotten the high EMF readings. Our first stop was a large bathroom. As I stepped inside the temperature read a comfortable 75 degrees, but in an instant dropped to only 42 degrees! The icy air mass certainly sent a chill up my spine, and for the first time that night we had some genuine screaming. The bitter cold presence was too much for some of the girls who yelled, "Let me out!" as they scrambled to get away from the tomb-like atmosphere. John recorded some more of the suspicious spots moving through the air with the camcorder, but again, they may have just been dust.

The next stop was a bedroom. There were some suspicious EMF readings, but the most interesting thing was what I can only describe as a "crackling" sound, for which we could find no source. I don't know what the significance could have been of that type of sound, other than it clearly stood out and caught our attention.

After the investigation, Claude told me that several people have experienced unusual things in that bedroom and adjoining bathroom, such as hearing footsteps on the stairs and hallway. One visitor from

Scotland thought he was alone in the house, until he heard a man coming up the stairs. He called out, "Claude, is that you?" thinking his host had returned, but there was no reply and the footsteps stopped.

Others have also heard the footsteps late at night, and after searching the house have found that no one else was there. One person staying in that bedroom had reported hearing three knocks, which is something significant to the Masons. So perhaps there are brother masons in spirit roaming around the house? Others have experienced a presence in the bathroom, and the faucet has turned on by itself.

It's important to note that none of these encounters have been malicious, although they were undoubtedly unnerving when the guests realized they just had a brush with the paranormal. Instead, it seems that one or more spirits are just curious about visitors, and want to leave unmistakable indications that this house is never empty.

There is a large room on the second floor that the Masons use for ceremonies, and it is set up with several large, majestic chairs. One day when two Masons were sitting in those chairs they saw a man walk down the hall and pass by the doorway. They both saw the same figure at the same time, but both men also knew that they were alone in the house. A subsequent search confirmed that, yet nothing could convince them that they had imagined the figure.

I found this room to be of particular interest—not that cold spots and EMF readings and footsteps aren't interesting—it was just that I felt a persistent and insistent attempt at contact here. This was more than just a display of paranormal energy, it was either a strong residual memory (a type of psychic imprint left on the room) or possibly a conscious effort to send a message.

As I've said many times in the past, I try to remain objective and stick to the rational and scientific approach to investigations. However, unless you have the sensitivity of a brick wall, you can't help but feel impressions, emotions and thoughts at such places. And after spending countless hours at dozens of haunted locations, your natural intuition becomes more sensitive and attuned to the dead. Whether or not that's a good thing remains to be seen…

In any event, in this room I kept getting the feeling that I was supposed to be finding something more, that there was important evidence to be discovered. I also had the strong sense that someone connected with this room had unfinished business when he died, which was perhaps why his spirit has been unable to rest.

Unfortunately, there was nothing specific, and a mass ghost hunt was not the time to pursue quiet contemplation on the subject. On the one hand, it was disappointingly vague, but then again, there is nothing mundane about thoughts from the other side touching your mind. Even now I can still recall that persistent sense of urgency to uncover some lost truth and finish a task that death interrupted.

Of course I still had quite a task ahead of me that night—the third floor had yet to be explored, and the entire basement was still awaiting us. I reluctantly left the large ceremonial room, and as I ascended the stairs the persistent thoughts faded, reinforcing, to my mind at least, that it was a localized phenomena (i.e., to that particular room, not the entire house).

The third floor had several rooms that needed to be refurbished, and it would not have been wise to pack a few dozen Girl Scouts in them. I poked around in each room, and John reported that, "things were flying around," on the infrared camcorder (those notorious white specks again).

The room of real interest—historically and paranormally—on this floor is the old Masonic meeting room that was added by John McGarrah in 1817. This is the oldest Masonic meeting room in the state of New York. And to think a car dealer wanted to tear down this place!

Benches lining the walls of this room were soon filled with Scouts. Claude took the seat at the head of the room, and I sat on the floor with my instruments. Several girls reported feeling a sense of anger, a presence that was "very mad" about something. Others felt a sadness, almost to the point of tears. I suggested we all try to remain quiet for a minute, with limited success, but there was an odd sound that came from one of the floors below.

Claude then related a story about giving a guest a tour. While in this room, he heard very heavy footsteps coming up both flights of stairs. Looking over at the guest, the man said, "I heard it, too." Not thinking that the loud and obvious footsteps were anything other than another visitor looking for them, Claude shouted, "We're up here."

There was no response. The footsteps came to an abrupt end and no one else could be found in the house. Over the years, several others have heard the heavy footsteps while in this old meeting room.

There were also small, narrow attics on the front and back ends of the house. The one in the back was actually more of a crawl space. I didn't venture in, as I wasn't sure of the condition of the floor, but even at the entrance there was an uncomfortable feeling. The front attic was more spacious, with a strong floor, and while checking it out we heard a loud pounding on the wall. I was certain it wasn't any of our group, because the sound was coming from the outside, three floors up! It only happened once, but that was enough to make an impression.

There were more surprises awaiting us in the basement, which consisted of several rooms. I went in alone first, just to get my bearings and to get a sense of the place before everyone piled in. There were high EMF readings in several places. When I came to the last room I heard a metallic banging sound, but couldn't see anything in the darkness. I switched on my flashlight and directed it in front of me and saw an old water heater type of tank about ten feet ahead.

I waited a moment for any other sounds, then approached the tank and knocked on it with my knuckles. The sound the tank produced was almost identical to the one I had heard when I entered the room, but how had it been produced? I was alone, or so I thought...

The noise level behind me started to grow so I knew everyone was in the first room of the basement, eagerly awaiting the final phase of the investigation. I made my way back to the group and quickly realized there were too many people to go through the basement all at once. I suggested a few at a time, but couldn't get let less than a dozen eager volunteers to go first.

Nothing unusual happened until we reached that back room. Right away we hit a cold spot. The entire basement was chilly, but there was one localized spot that was bitter cold, disturbingly cold. I suggested we form a circle around the spot, and a chill passed through all of us as we surrounded the area that was roughly two or three feet in diameter. I placed the EMF in the center of the spot, and the readings shot up. There was clearly a strong energy there, paranormal or not—although my money was on paranormal, and I was willing to give ten to one odds.

I asked if there was anything particularly unusual about this room, and Claude pointed out that the stone foundation was not the same here as the rest of the basement. Apparently, the old inn had been built on an even older foundation, and who knows what could have taken place in that original 18th century structure?

While there was no way to tell what had happened in the past, there was no mistaking what was going on in the present. Something else was in the blackness of the basement with us, and I was impressed that all those Girl Scouts held their ground and didn't run away.

A faint light from the front of the basement made its way down the hall, just bright enough that I could see Claude's silhouette in the doorway. As I continued to check EMF and temperature readings, I occasionally glanced over to the doorway and saw the outline of Claude's figure, which was shortly joined by another, slightly taller dark silhouette. I assumed that it was one of the parents, and kept taking readings and photos. At least three times I looked toward the doorway and distinctly saw two men standing there.

Still thinking nothing of it, as so many people were there that night, I didn't focus on the doorway until I heard a long, deep sigh. It was not simply a long exhale, it was full of emotion and I wondered why Claude, or the man behind him, was upset. When I looked toward the doorway again, I only saw one figure, and I asked Claude if he had just sighed. He replied that he had not. I asked about the man behind him, and he replied that there had *not* been another person behind him, that he had been alone in the hallway the entire time! However, he had heard noises directly behind him three times and each time he turned to look but saw nothing.

Now I was *really* impressed with this place! As fascinating as noises, cold spots and EMF readings are, they literally pale in comparison to a good dark and solid apparition! We all heard the plaintive sigh (which sounded like it came from a man) and I clearly saw a second figure standing behind Claude for at least a couple of minutes. This was not a fleeting glimpse out of the corner of my eye. He appeared to be so real that I didn't realize he was unreal—and I never thought to take a picture of him!

Was this one of the men that had been seen wandering the halls, or heard climbing the stairs? Was this John McGarrah, a family member, a former guest of the inn, or a Mason? Or was this dark entity connected with the earlier structure that stood here before the inn was built? He obviously had some particular interest in this room, and had the energy to create sounds, generate a strong cold spot and make a sustained and bold appearance. Too bad he didn't use all that energy to remove himself from this location and move on to some better place!

At this point, other groups of Scouts wanted their turn in the back room of the basement. While there were a few things of interest that occurred with the other groups, nothing matched the dark, sighing spirit. After everyone had their turn, we all met upstairs at the long tables in the dining area. We went over the events of the evening, and Claude related more stories of the history and the haunting of McGarrah's Inn.

It was an amazing evening. I began the night with low expectations, and left with some of the most impressive paranormal experiences I've ever had. I also left with something I never before received—a patch of McGarrah's Inn given to the Girl Scouts to commemorate this night! How cool is that, a ghost hunting merit badge?

Claude had offered to have me come back again, so we arranged an evening in July of 2006. The original plan was for it to be a quiet, more controlled investigation, but you know what they say about plans...

Claude suggested asking Hudson Valley's News 12 if they would be interested in covering the investigation, and I welcomed the idea of inviting the media. As my "mission," as it were, is to gather credible evidence and present it to the public, what better way than to have the television cameras rolling?

Of course, if you're going to have reporters doing a story, you need people to interview—and who better than the Girl Scouts (note the plural) who have been experiencing strange things at the old inn. And of course, the Scouts needed parents (note the plural) to drive them there.

I wasn't fully aware of all the arrangements that had taken place in the brief twenty-four hours from first speaking to the News 12 producer to the scheduled start of the ghost hunt. So as I headed to McGarrah's that evening I was still in the mindset that after a brief interview, I was basically going to be alone in the old house in a silent, solo investigation. Reality hit as I turned into the driveway and saw that the parking lot was full of cars and people!

It just goes to show you can't keep a good ghost story down! I was actually glad to have the opportunity to speak with the Scouts and parents again to get an update on what had been occurring in the months since I had been there. Among the many things that continue to go bump in the night was one very curious item—a toilet that apparently flushes on its own. Haunted toilets; now *there* was a novelty! However, I quickly set aside all thoughts of possessed plumbing as I prepared the equipment for the investigation.

The new plan was for the reporter, Dianna Russini, to interview all the Scouts, then they would leave and it would just be me, Claude, Dianna and the cameraman, Stephen O'Leary. It would be interesting to see how the News 12 people would handle a haunted house, as I have on more than one occasion in the past watched reporters and crew members scream and run. Perhaps nothing would happen, and perhaps they would get more of a story than they bargained for...

Before beginning the investigation, Claude related an interesting story. One of the men who had experienced strange things in the house contacted a psychic medium in California. He told her about what was going on in the house, and she said that the spirits did not like having all the doors closed. If the doors were kept open throughout the house, the activity would diminish.

Deciding they had nothing to lose by trying, they opened the doors, and indeed the level of activity appeared to decrease. Of course, the story made us all think the same thing—let's close all of the doors and see if we can stir things up! While I never do anything aimed at really annoying the spirit world, I certainly don't object to giving the invisible inhabitants some incentive to providing clear evidence, so we started closing doors.

Just as we were about to start shooting, Steve had problems with the battery pack on his camera. It was fully charged, but didn't seem to

An infrared image of News 12 reporter Dianna Russini and cameraman Stephen O'Leary in the kitchen of McGarrah's.

work right away. Once that was resolved, we started moving from room to room. Nothing unusual happened until we were in the front parlor, sitting quietly in the dark. I said that if anything wanted to make its presence known, now was the time. We sat, we listened, we waited—nothing.

I was about to suggest moving on to the next room, until I glanced down at the EMF meter I had placed in my lap. By the light of

Steve's camera, I saw that there was a fairly high reading of 1.8. It had read zero when we first sat down, and remained at zero for several minutes, which is why I put it down on my lap. I sat perfectly still watching the meter to see if it was just a temporary spike, but it held steady just below two. A bit of a chill went up my spine, but I calmly reported that I was getting anomalous readings. The camera zoomed into the meter and the reading held steady. Something was creating a measurable energy field around me.

Next came that small storage room where I had the high EMF readings the last time. This time there was nothing—but later in the evening the high readings had returned. Go figure…

The kitchen held no surprises, and I was beginning to think that the News 12 segment would be very short and uneventful. However, the spirits of the old house had some startling surprises in store for us.

We sat in the upstairs bedroom where several different visitors over the years had reported hearing very loud and clear footsteps ascending the stairs (its adjacent bathroom was the site of the allegedly haunted toilet, and a measurable cold spot during the first investigation). Claude sat on the bed in the middle of the room, Dianna sat in the corner near the closet door to Claude's right, I was on the opposite side of the room, and Steve was a couple of feet to my right, near a window.

We waited to see if there were any footsteps, but nothing happened—at first. Then as Claude was relating a story about the house, there was suddenly a very distinct and spine-tingling sound. I thought it came from the hallway, Steve thought it came from behind him by the window, Dianna wasn't sure where it came from, and Claude didn't hear it. But the three of us who did hear it agreed on one thing—it was unmistakably a man moaning.

It startled me, and the News 12 reporter and cameraman were admittedly scared, but I have to say they held their ground. And given the nature of the terrible and unnerving moan, staying put was no small feat. I believe it takes considerable energy to create that kind of intense utterance, so whatever entity was behind this was certainly not weak.

It was also most certainly not happy. Had it been a laugh, a whisper, or just a normal voice, one could assume that a spirit was just trying to make its presence known. However, with a moan or cry of such anguish and torment you can only draw two conclusions—something was trying to frighten us with the worst sound it could muster, or this spirit was trying to convey its suffering. Either way, these were not comforting thoughts.

(The moan was definitely different from the sad sigh in the basement, although they both sounded like they were from a man, and both were filled with emotion. I obviously couldn't say whether or not they had been produced by the same entity, but I would keep that thought in mind for any future investigations.)

We waited for some time to see if the moaning would repeat, but there was only silence. Steve was recording audio on his camera at the time, and he did pick up the bizarre sound, but it is faint, and partially covered by Claude's voice. While I was hoping for a clear recording, this does indicate that the sound was not near the camera, but more likely beyond the closed bedroom door out in the hall, or perhaps the bathroom. And since we were the only four living people in the house, this makes for one incredible piece of evidence. Unimaginably frightening, of course, but incredible.

We decided to check out the bathroom next. Dianna was brave enough to go in with me, and when we closed the door it became so dark you could barely see a thing. She slowly scanned the room with the infrared camcorder as we stood practically breathless straining to hear the slightest noise. After the disturbing moaning sound we had heard, I had high hopes that we would hear or see something equally as impressive in the bathroom, but all was quiet—until we gave up and started to leave.

Just as we were crossing the threshold back into the bedroom, the toilet flushed by itself. Fortunately, Steve caught the incident on camera. Dianna and I were both by the doorway—at least ten feet from the toilet—so it clearly could not have been either of us pushing the handle. Can you imagine being in an old haunted house with all your senses on high alert as you feel your way through the blackness, and suddenly a toilet flushes behind your back! It was so startling we both gasped, but nobody panicked. Steve kept shooting, and as Dianna was holding the camcorder, I pointed to the toilet and said to her, "Get it! Get it!" She hurried back inside and was able to record the swirling water on tape.

Of course, we had to find out from Claude if there were any plumbing problems, and he said there hadn't been any. And while it's possible for seals to not fit properly and for the water to keep running, an actual flush is rather unusual, to say the least. And believe me, it was with mixed emotions that I viewed this bizarre event. On the one hand, it was possibly one of the most fascinating paranormal occurrences I had witnessed. On the other hand, in the next couple of days the entire Hudson Valley would be seeing me with a haunted toilet!

Oh well, they say there's no such thing as bad publicity...

The News 12 segment showed the infamous toilet flushing scene. Dianna had just exited the bathroom and I was in the doorway when the toilet flushed. Here, you can see Dianna quickly turning at the sound, and the surprised look in my eyes as I start to turn back. (The caption is a bar that constantly shows headlines and weather information throughout the program.)

However, there is disingenuous publicity, and I must set the record straight on something. When the segment aired, they showed a door seemingly open on its own, with me looking very surprised. That did happen, but not as portrayed, and it was for perfectly natural reasons.

When we were first in the bedroom with the door closed, I opened the bathroom door to check it out with the meter. My back was to the bedroom door, and it was dark, so I didn't see that the bedroom door had slowly and silently opened. Both Claude and Steve saw it move as if by invisible hands, and told me what happened. I quickly turned around and was indeed surprised to see the door standing open. This was shown on TV, along with the door actually opening as if they caught it in the act.

It made for a great scene in the show, but the truth was that as soon as I saw the open bedroom door, I examined it and found there wasn't a latch. I closed both doors, and with the camera running I opened the bathroom door. The change in air pressure caused the bedroom door to swing open at the same time. I repeated this several times just to prove it was natural air pressure, not a supernatural force, at work, but one of those scenes was used for the mysterious opening door segment.

Sorry News12, for exposing the trick, but all I need is for word to get out that I took part in staging evidence. It's hard enough trying to maintain credibility as a ghost investigator—let alone a ghost investigator with a haunted toilet—so I just had to explain what really happened.

We continued on to the next floor and spent some time in the old meeting room with the arched ceiling. We all sat in different parts of the room, and almost immediately there was a tapping sound from the corner of the room where Steve was sitting. We all heard it and thought it was just Steve tapping on the wooden bench, or moving his feet. However, in the dim light it looked to me that he was perfectly still, so I asked him if he was somehow making that noise. He quickly replied that it wasn't him, and he wasn't moving a muscle. The tapping was somewhere in the corner, about three or four feet to his left, and he clearly wasn't happy about it.

I moved closer and was able to verify the location of the sound, if not its source. When I was only a few feet away there were several other sounds indicating something was moving, but nothing could be seen. I sat in the corner for several minutes, but the sounds stopped and I couldn't find anything that would have caused them.

The News 12 people were certainly getting a good idea of the nature of ghost hunting—a lot of questions, few answers, and you never knew what would happen at any given second. To be sure, plenty was happening, but how or why the bizarre things were occurring was impossible to say, although it seemed as though there were several different spirits with different messages to convey.

There was still one area of the house to explore, and on the first investigation it had produced some very interesting messages—the old basement, which had produced high EMF readings, strange sounds and a shadowy figure. I was anxious to see what was in store for us this time!

As we stood in the darkness of the back room of the basement, I asked if anything wanted to make its presence known. Almost immediately there was a sound. It did not originate near us in the basement, but came from above us—two floors above us, to be precise. It was the mystery toilet flushing again! This was just getting too weird...

And it got weirder. Later I asked for another sign, and again the toilet flushed. Even if someone else had been hiding in the house, there was no way they could have known to time the flushing so exactly to my request. Dianna suggested that perhaps it was a plumbing problem, and that it went off on its own on a regular basis. A good idea, but it had been an hour between the time we heard it for the first time when we were leaving the bathroom, and then the second time when we heard it in the basement, but only seven minutes between the second time and then the third. Still, I would continue to look for a pattern just in case.

(Note to potential ghost hunters: How did I know it was seven minutes? By habit I frequently check my watch during an investigation, especially when something notable happens. When you are considering what equipment to buy, don't forget a good watch that is self-illuminated. There are those that light up when you push a button, but with all the other equipment to carry, you rarely have a free hand. I wear a Luminox, which has clear and bright hands and hour markers.)

Despite being in a creepy basement in a haunted house, this whole toilet thing was becoming quite amusing. In fact, twenty-one minutes later, I said out loud, "This is your last chance to give us some sign of your presence. Do something to let us know you're here."

I'll give you three guesses as to what happened just seconds later, although I'll bet you only need one. Yes, the infamous second floor toilet came through again. When I checked the videotape, I found it was only three seconds from the time I said, "Do something to let us know you're here," to the flushing sound. Steve turned on his camera, and there I am laughing and saying, "This is uncanny. (No pun intended.) Do you believe this?" It was indeed hard to believe, and if I didn't have it on tape I might begin to doubt my own memory.

That was the last time we were to hear the toilet it that night—maybe because I stopped asking for signs, and maybe because whatever it was had more than proven its point. In fact after that, we were in the house for over an hour longer, and nothing else happened.

Top photo: An infrared image of me in the darkness of the basement as I am about to ask for a sign that spirits are in the house.

Bottom photo: Just seconds later the toilet flushed, and Steve turned on the camera light to film my reaction.

The segment aired on News 12 two days later, and while I had been prepared for some good-natured ribbing about the toilet scene, I only received positive feedback. The way it was presented clearly evoked more fear than laughs, perhaps in part because you can see we are obviously startled by the event.

Immediately after the segment, one of the newscasters commented that she was skeptical and felt that the house simply needed a good plumber. That would be a rational response and would seem to make sense—unless you had been in the dark basement and heard the toilet flush—twice—in response to your request for a sign of the spirits' presence. The timing was just too precise for this to have been a coincidence.

And let us not forget that awful moan! Believe me, it was loud, clear and shocking. I've had more than my share of frightening paranormal voices (the Death Breath, the woman's scream in my car, etc.), and this was right up there for clarity and impact.

Of all the things that transpired during my two investigations of the old McGarrah's Inn, the moan was perhaps the most astonishing, although the dark figure in the basement is a close second. It would have been number one if I had realized at the time that I was not looking at a living human being!

What can I conclude from all the sights, sounds, energy readings and eyewitness accounts? This is one very haunted house, with numerous entities prowling its dark corners. It is definitely a location to which I would like to return—this time spending the entire night with equipment running throughout the house and basement.

Again, I must applaud Claude Horstmann's efforts to preserve this wonderful historic structure. And I think the car dealer who wanted to knock it down should also thank Claude, as I bet he would have ended up with one creepy car lot…

Gomez Mill House

The Gomez Mill House

It never ceases to amaze me how many "coincidences" I encounter. This story involves a prime example, which began at a rest stop in New York on the way to the Rolling Hills Asylum in July of 2006.

You know those ubiquitous racks of travel brochures, usually standing just inside the entrance to practically every roadside rest stop in America? Well, I'm a travel brochure junkie, always looking for information on interesting things to do and places to go. On this particular stop near Rochester, I found *New York State Revolutionary War Heritage Trail*, a really nice publication that had a map of the historic points of interest relating to the Revolution, and small pictures and descriptions of the various sites.

One place caught my eye in particular—the Gomez Mill House in Marlboro, New York, just about half an hour from where I live. I had heard of it, but didn't know anything of its history, and I said to Mike that I would like to visit it someday. I even wondered if such an old place might be haunted...

When I returned from that trip, I had a long list of emails awaiting me. One email in particular caught my eye—it was from an employee of the Gomez Mill House wondering if I would have any interest in investigating the ghostly activity there!

I kid you not, ladies and gentleman, this is how bizarre my life is (and that's only the tip of the iceberg...).

Fate was apparently pointing its finger, if not giving me a shove, so I quickly arranged to go just a few days later. However, before I describe the ghostly aspects of the Gomez Mill House, I will risk sounding like a travel brochure to relate the incredible history of the place.

It all began in Spain in 1660, when Luis Moses Gomez was born into a wealthy Jewish family with close ties to the royal court. Life should have been good for the boy, except for the resurgence of a nasty little thing called the Inquisition. The Spanish Inquisition was arguably the nastiest of them all, and it basically consisted of allegedly devout and God-loving Catholics torturing and murdering anyone who didn't agree with their beliefs—and Jews were prime targets.

The family fled to France, and over the next forty years Luis Gomez traveled far and wide, finally settling in New York City. The Gomez family became the richest and most influential Jewish family in America at the time, but Luis was not content to rest on his fortune. In 1714, he bought a large piece of land on the Hudson River so he could build an Indian trading post.

Ironically, the land included a former Indian ceremonial site known as the Danskammer. (The Dutch, frightened by the sight of a large Indian ceremony held there one night, called it "de Dans Kamer van de Duyfel"—the "Devil's Dance Chamber.") Now the Indians returned to the land that they once held sacred to trade furs in exchange for trinkets, guns and rum.

However, both the dwindling Indian and fur-bearing animal populations made the trading post obsolete in just twenty years. The simple one-room trading post was to undergo several expansions over the centuries in the hands of some interesting owners. Wolvert Acker, a staunch patriot, bought the place in 1772 and added a second story and a large attic. In 1835, the Armstrong family purchased the property, and Edward Armstrong added a fine mansion on the Danskammer overlooking the river.

The original room that Luis Gomez built in 1714 as a trading post. People claim that the eyes of the women in the portrait follow you around the room.

In general, life was very good for the wealthy, talented and adventurous Armstrong family, but one poignant tragedy hung like a dark cloud over their lives. In 1873, the bright and energetic five-year-old Emily Armstrong was playing near the mill creek in front of the house. She had been running and playing with her dog, Twist, when she fell and hit her head on a rock. Her lifeless body was found face down in the creek, and legend has it that Twist died shortly after of a broken heart. Though the family lived there for another thirty years, they never fully recovered from their terrible loss.

The stream where little Emily Armstrong died in 1873. The water level is very low in his photo, but you can see by the exposed roots that it gets much deeper.

Emily is buried in a cemetery down the road. Her dog, Twist, is buried near the rock wall in front of the house.

The next owner was craftsman Dard Hunter, who built a quaint-looking paper mill on the creek. He would make his handmade paper in the mill, then hang the sheets to dry in the attic. The Hunters attracted an artistic crowd, and many famous people, including furniture designer Gustav Stickley, regularly visited the old mill house.

The mill that Dard Hunter constructed.

The last, and arguably the most important private owner since Luis Gomez, bought the place after World War II, when America entered a baby and building boom. Historic structures were being torn down for new housing developments, and Mildred Starin didn't want to see that happen to this magnificent house. Her philosophy was that while "striving for the new, we should cherish and protect the old," and through her efforts the Gomez Mill Hose was preserved and protected by entering it into the National Register of Historic Places in 1973.

Mildred also contacted family members of former owners, and brought back many important pieces of these families' histories to the house, such as Wolvert Acker's Bible box, documents, paintings and artifacts. The second part of her plan was to open the house to the public, which was accomplished when the Gomez Mill Foundation was formed and bought the property in 1984.

Today, the oldest Jewish residence in America, and the home of patriots, entrepreneurs, adventurers, artists and preservationists is open to the public for tours, lectures, classes and events. It may also have an open door to the other world...

As I drove to Marlboro that record setting, hot and humid summer's day (a bank thermometer read 101 degrees, and the heat index was hovering around 115), I again marveled at the extraordinary timing of first thinking about visiting the house and then finding the invitation when I got home. As I pulled onto Mill House Road and first glimpsed the old structure, I marveled at the beauty of the place and tried to imagine what it was like in 1714 when Indians traded here, or even earlier, before the settlers arrived. It's always fascinating to investigate such historic sites, and I'm more than content to just learn of the people and events, even if there aren't any ghosts. But ghosts were what I was there for, so I grabbed my gear and knocked on the door.

I was greeted by Angela-Rose Simmons, who had decided to contact me as she had read a couple of my *Haunted Hudson Valley* books. Angela-Rose has been working in the house since April, along with Crystal Hughes, and they have experienced several unusual things in their short time there. They also had interesting stories to relate from a former employee, Jane Healy, who seemed to be particularly sensitive to the spirits who may still walk the halls.

We began in the office—the only air conditioned section of the house—where I also met Site Manager Ellen Healy, who has been working at the Gomez Mill House for eleven years. One of her personal experiences with inexplicable phenomena is the smell of cigar smoke. She has detected the odor of cigars on numerous occasions, often in the kitchen, even though no one else is in the building and there's a strict no smoking rule.

Ellen also said that a visitor season has never passed when at least one person hasn't made some comment about the place being haunted. One year a nun came up to her and asked if she knew if any babies had died on the property. An odd question, but it became even odder when the nun went on to say she had asked because she saw the spirits of two babies over the millpond. (Dard Hunter's wife had a stillborn baby, and of course there could have been many others over the course of three hundred years.)

Several years ago there was a fire, and the firemen who responded claimed that the place was haunted, and that they "got slimed," whatever that means! (Perhaps this was near the time of the *Ghostbusters* movie.) Apparently it was no joke, as they later went to a priest to get blessed and sprinkled with holy water. To this day, one of the firemen still refuses to set foot back in the house. (It should be pointed out that he was also a prominent local politician, with nothing to gain by spreading stories of being attacked by ghosts.)

One afternoon during this past winter, Jane was cleaning the main staircase, when suddenly the door beneath the stairs swung open. There is just a small, enclosed storage space under the stairs, so she couldn't understand why the door would open on its own. She came down the stairs and closed it, but it forcefully swung open again. Stepping back, she looked up at the stairs, and there, right in front of her, was the face of a small boy with an old-fashioned Dutch boy haircut, peering at her from between the balusters of the railing!

Terrified, she ran to the office to get Ellen. By the time the two women returned, the boy had disappeared. However, as Jane was describing what she had seen, the storage door swung open again, sending both women running.

In April, Angela-Rose was cleaning up by the visitor's center (a small building adjacent to the house) when she heard voices across the street at the mill. She could tell that a man and a woman were talking, and she decided to see if she could be of any assistance to them and provide some information on the place. As she crossed the street, she looked all around for the people, but couldn't see them. Reaching the mill, she still couldn't find the man and the woman who she had so clearly heard talking, and never found any explanation for the voices.

Later that same day, Angela-Rose, Crystal and Jane heard strange static coming over the walkie-talkies, even though no one was transmitting with them. Then they heard a woman's voice. It was garbled, and Angela-Rose and Crystal couldn't make out the words, but Jane was certain she heard the woman say, "Get out of my house!"

The door that opened on its own, and the stairs where the little boy appeared.

For the most part, paranormal activity in the house is benign, and occasionally mischievous, but the kitchen has a different feeling to it. Kitchens are often the warmest and most inviting rooms in a house, but not here. There is a hostile, unpleasant, "get out of my house" feeling to it.

One day, several members of the staff were in the kitchen when the light fixture started swinging back and forth. Angela-Rose took hold of it and stopped the motion. A few minutes later, they all had their backs to the fixture, and when they turned they saw that it had started swinging again. They thought that perhaps someone walking on the floor above them could have caused a vibration that set it in motion, but they realized that they were the only ones in the house.

That same day, Jane was alone in the hallway leading to the kitchen and someone yanked her hair. Later, she suffered a nosebleed, for no apparent reason. Perhaps it's a good thing that she doesn't work there any longer!

The kitchen light fixture that started swinging.

Another incident involving the kitchen occurred one day when Angela-Rose was outside. She looked through the kitchen window and saw a figure—she thought it might be Jane—and waved to her. The person did not acknowledge the greeting and turned away. When Angela-Rose came into the house, she was surprised that no one was in the kitchen. She later found out that no one had been in the kitchen that day.

Can this unpleasant entity in the kitchen be identified? Is it possible to determine who was the little boy on the staircase? With almost three centuries of human habitation (and probably many hundreds more of Native American settlements), it's hard to say for certain what tragic event or trapped soul is responsible for specific activities, but there may be one instance that can be related to a particular individual.

Angela-Rose was alone cleaning the upstairs bedroom of a former owner who once ran a school in the house. As she was about to exit the room she saw that the antique rocking horse in the hall was rocking back and forth. She looked on in disbelief as the horse moved on its own, and Angela-Rose could have sworn she heard a child laughing. Then, just as she crossed the threshold from the bedroom into the hall, the horse abruptly stopped moving and became perfectly still, as if some strange spell had been broken.

Was this a sign from the child who once owned this horse? If it was, then we know both who it was, and how the child died, for this rocking horse belonged to Emily Armstrong, who tragically lost her life on the property in 1873!

Recently, Crystal and Ellen welcomed a group who had arrived for a tour. They generally show people a video about the history of the place in the Visitor's Center before actually taking them through the house. The video began, and Crystal and Ellen left to take care of some work in the house while the tape was running. Almost immediately, they heard the bathroom door slam shut, which has a distinctive sound that can easily be distinguished from the other doors in the house.

A few minutes later, they heard the bathroom door close again, then again. This was puzzling, as no one else could have entered the house undetected, as there are loud chimes on the entrance door so they can hear whenever anyone comes inside. Crystal went to check on what was going on, but no one was in the bathroom. A few minutes later, that same bathroom door closed hard again. This time Ellen went to investigate and also found no one around.

Still thinking it must somehow have been one of the visitors slamming the bathroom door, Crystal began her tour by saying, "I don't want to be rude, but did any of you use the bathroom several times?"

Emily's rocking horse.

No one in the group had left the Visitor's Center, and, as no one else was in the house, this incident remains a mystery.

There was another incident involving this bathroom a few weeks later. Crystal and another employee, Meghan, were alone in the house and getting ready to close up. Crystal's father arrived to drive her home, and he asked to use the bathroom. She told him where it was, and a few moments later he called to her, saying the water was running. Thinking he meant the toilet was running, she told him to just jiggle the handle. He replied it wasn't the toilet, it was the sink.

Crystal went to see what he was talking about, and sure enough, the faucet had been turned on and water was streaming into the sink. Neither she nor Meghan had turned on the water in that bathroom, so the mystery of that room only deepened.

There is yet another mystery that may be related to this property. According to records, at least one former owner had slaves. These records also show that one the slaves died horribly—burned at the stake, to be exact—although it isn't clear if this actually happened on the property, and it also isn't known why this slave was killed in this manner. (It is ironic to think such a thing could happen to someone in America, when this was precisely why the Gomez family had fled Spain and the Inquisition.) Such a torturous death could certainly make for one unhappy spirit, but it is all speculation until further evidence can be uncovered.

During my brief tour/investigation, I was fascinated with the house and grounds, and with the stories of the people connected to this place. While I didn't see the apparition of a mischievous little boy, or witness any doors opening on their own, there was a palpable feeling about the place. Actually, there were several feelings of distinct personalities in various sections of the house. And I do have to agree that the kitchen has a totally different feel to it, and not a pleasant one, at that.

Of course, feelings are not objective evidence, and I clearly recognize that. However, my EMF meter does not have any feelings, and it produced some tantalizing results. Angela-Rose, Crystal and I were sitting quietly in the hallway that contains the rocking horse, and the meter was on the couch next to me. The display read zero, as it had throughout the investigation, until we started talking about the activity that had taken place in this area. Slowly, the readings climbed—0.4, 0.7, 1.2, 1.8, and then held steady around 2.0.

There was no external reason for this energy field. I didn't move or even touch the meter, and there wasn't any natural electrical source nearby. The only thing that had happened was that we started talking about the ghosts in this hallway, and suddenly a measurable energy field appeared. It lasted over a minute, and then slowly diminished. We waited a while, but it did not return. Perhaps it wasn't the most dramatic thing that could have happened that day, but when you have investigated several dozen haunted locations, you know a paranormal sign when you see one!

This had just been a basic "walk-through" investigation, where I interview witnesses, get familiar with a location, and determine if an extensive investigation is warranted. Given the multiple, independent eyewitnesses over the years, and the long history of the place, I would definitely place the Gomez Mill House near the top of my haunted "Wish List" of places to return and examine in-depth, and overnight.

As always, I encourage you to explore on your own. Even if there wasn't ever a single thing that went bump in the night here, it is well worth the trip to see a precious piece of American history. And if some unseen hand does pull your hair, or you see the peering face of a little boy, it will simply add another dimension to your visit—a dimension of the sixth sense that flows strongly through the three centuries-old Gomez Mill House.

To arrange a tour, call (845) 236-3126 or go to www.gomez.org

Angela-Rose and Crystal on the couch where there were high EMF readings. Note the rocking horse in the corner.

Rolling Hills

Asylums are not happy places. So when Mike suggested going to the former Rolling Hills Asylum in Bethany, New York, I had mixed feelings. It was a great opportunity to conduct a large-scale investigation in what was reputedly a very haunted location. On the other hand, my unpleasant experiences during an investigation at a mental hospital a few years ago (See *GI Vol. 3*) were still fresh in my mind. Of course, unpleasant things are part of the territory for a ghost investigator, so naturally I agreed to go.

The history of Rolling Hills stretches back to the 1700s when a stagecoach inn and tavern operated on the site. This property was on a major thoroughfare (which eventually became Route 20) for travelers passing through western New York, up until the New York State Thruway was constructed in the mid-twentieth century.

The nature of the inn would change dramatically in 1827 from a place where people would gladly spend the night, to a place where people reluctantly spent the rest of their lives. In 1824 the state passed a law that placed the burden of taking care of the poor on counties, rather than individual towns, and Genesee County chose the stagecoach property for its poorhouse. Over the years, the list of occupants grew to include the physically sick, the mentally ill, drunks, unwed mothers, orphans and just about everybody else who wasn't able to take care of themselves.

It's a nice idea to think that, regardless of your circumstances, there is somewhere you can go to have a roof over your head and something to eat. The reality was that Rolling Hills became terribly overcrowded, there was widespread abuse, and the terminally ill and criminally insane were crammed into the same rooms (sometimes even the same beds!) with defenseless children and pregnant women. More than 1,000 deaths within the walls of this asylum have been officially recorded, but the countless untold horrors will never be known.

Over the decades, new buildings were erected and residents worked on the asylum's farms to feed the growing numbers of the sick and destitute. Tuberculosis patients began coming to Rolling Hills, and usually never left. As the twentieth century progressed, different segments of the asylum's population were sent to specialized facilities, and by the 1950s, Rolling Hills was strictly a nursing home for the elderly. In 1974, the last residents had been relocated and the doors to the asylum were closed.

> Jan 29, 1886
>
> **FIFTY-EIGHT YEARS IN THE POOR HOUSE.**—Miss Phebe White was found dead in her room in the County House on Sunday morning last. She was 67 years of age. For 58 years she had been an inmate, never having spent a single night away from that institution. The County House was completed in 1827 and Miss White entered it at 9 years of age in 1828, thus becoming one of the first recipients of its care and protection. She was always idiotic, and for the past ten years she has been totally blind. She had some musical talent and could whistle or hum a tune after hearing it once or twice. Her personal habits were filthy beyond all description, which made her a great care and burden. Miss White is a distant relative of the Ben White who was hung in Batavia in 1843. Superintendent Hay, in looking over the books of the poor house, estimates her cost to the county during the 58 years at $7,000, and this amount would not begin to pay for the trouble she has made if an attendant had been hired to care for her. Why such persons are permitted to be a burden so many years, while scores of beautiful lives come to an early end, is one of the mysteries that will never be solved in this life.

This obituary of lifelong inmate Phebe White is not only devoid of compassion, it is cruel. If this is how they spoke about her after her death, how was she treated in life?

For almost twenty years Rolling Hills stood vacant—at least of living occupants. Then in the early 1990s the property was sold and part of the main building was opened as Carriage Village Shops. There was even an attempt to turn one wing into apartments, but that plan was fortunately abandoned. (Can you imagine—"Would you like our two-bedroom Electroshock Treatment Suite, or would you prefer a one-bedroom in Solitary Confinement or the Morgue?")

In 2002, the remaining buildings and property were purchased by Jeff and Lori Carlson. Renamed the Rolling Hills Country Mall, there are currently dozens of craft and antique stores, a café, and the headquarters of the Rolling Hills Ghost Hunting Society. A rather unique combination! I don't think there are too many places where you can shop, have a bite to eat and then hunt for ghosts!

The main building of the former asylum.

Our investigation took place in April 2006, and due to scheduling constraints the only way we were able to go was to drive up in the afternoon, conduct the investigation, then head back in the wee hours of the morning. I do not handle sleep deprivation well, and the prospect of a 600-mile round trip was equally unappealing, but if Mike was willing to tackle the drive, it was an offer I couldn't refuse.

I met Mike in Port Jervis, NY, and we packed his SUV full of equipment. After picking up his brother, Scott, and friend, Marge, we headed for Bethany—through 300 miles of rolling farmland, an occasional city and a whole lot of nothing. At one of the rest stops I picked up some travel brochures (a good investigator always needs to stay informed!) and read about things to do in Genessee County. It was a relatively short list, but we all had a good laugh pondering whether we should cancel the ghost hunt and visit the Jell-O Gallery in Leroy, NY instead. (Hey, if you have the birthplace of one of America's favorite gelatinous desserts, flaunt it!)

When we finally hit Bethany, we stopped for dinner and a short rest before arriving at the old asylum just after dark. I had expected an enormous complex of large buildings, and was surprised to see just one moderate-sized structure that I recognized from the website photos. However, looks were deceiving, as I was to find that the building was enormous (65,000 sq.ft.) and stretched out into a disorienting array of wings, staircases, tunnels and more rooms than I could count.

Many of the old farm buildings that stood on the property no longer exist.

We met with Lori Carlson and she showed us the museum room that contains some artifacts and documents on the history of the place. It's always very important to know as much as you can about the people and events connected to a haunted location—especially in a remarkable case such as this—and I applaud Lori's efforts to gather the history of Rolling Hills. It is quite possible that among the various papers and photos there are vital clues to the restless spirits that wander the long, dark hallways.

The faces of two unknown residents from 1964. Could these be the faces of some of the ghosts?

The men's infirmary.

Curiously, for the first month of the new ghost hunting season (the place is closed in the winter due to the staggering amount of lake-effect snow), it appeared as though the spirits had been resting quite comfortably as everything had been unusually quiet. But wouldn't you know it, as soon as we arrived things started to go bump—and bang—

in the night. This wasn't the first time Mike and I had heard that our arrival had stirred up things. I'm beginning to think half these ghosts are just in it for the publicity!

Some members of the Rolling Hills Ghost Hunting Society were there and one of their members, Kirk, gave us all a quick tour of the place. There were three floors in two different wings that had branching corridors and front staircases and back staircases all shrouded in total darkness, and I was beginning to think I would have to set down a trail of road flares to get my bearings. I generally have a very good sense of direction, but with each floor and hallway basically looking like the next, it was difficult to establish landmarks by which to navigate. Lori and Kirk assured us that people who have been there a dozen times still get lost, so I didn't feel too bad.

Some of the "highlights" of the tour were the morgue, where the outlines of the grisly instruments that once hung along the wall could still be seen. There also used to be a collection of limbs hanging in this room (of the artifical variety) that were removed from the deceased owner and "recycled" for the living.

Then there were the chains still bolted to the walls of several rooms where unruly residents would be restrained. There was the wing where horrible electroshock treatments were administered, along with experimental treatments that often amounted to nothing less than torture. The solitary confinement chamber had been relabeled as the oxygen storage room, but the word "Detention" was still visible on the door. The nurses' dining area was at the end of this hall, so they must have heard all kinds of yelling and screams of torment as they ate. Not the best aid to digestion...

There were creepy underground tunnels that led to various outbuildings on the property. A photo in the museum shows workers trying to dig down through the snow that stood higher than a man, so it isn't surprising that given the severity of the winters these tunnels were essential for staff to be able to move between buildings.

Down one of these dark tunnels is the woodshop, where a man in his seventies has been seen wearing a tan shirt, a brown vest and brown work pants. He appears quite normal going about his business in the woodshop, but then he disappears quite abnormally—or paranormally, to be more precise.

Another lower level room is known as the Christmas Room, as year-round it's decorated for the holidays. This is where Santa sits and listens to local children tell him what's on their wish lists. But other children appear to be attracted to this room, or at least the spirits of children who place their tiny cold hands into the hands of the living, sing softly, and move objects. An experiment conducted by some ghost hunters involved placing toys in precise locations on a grid. They left the room and locked the door, and when they returned they found that the toys had been moved!

Don't let the lace curtains fool you—the metal brackets under the window were used to chain unruly patients.

This room was once used for solitary confinement. The word "Detention" over the window has been scratched out, and the word "Oxygen" stenciled on the door when its use changed. This was where the most violent and unmanageable were held.

As the tour progressed, we learned about other apparitions that have been sighted by the meat locker, a boiler room and various locations throughout the building. Of particular note is the figure of an old women sitting on a ground floor porch, often witnessed by people just driving by who are unaware of the haunted reputation of the place. It's believed that she also makes her presence known in the solarium at that end of the building. She is seen with such frequency that she is referred to by name—Maude—and has become a "regular" at Rolling Hills.

Other inexplicable phenomena include an old piano that plays by itself (it is not a player piano), doors that slam closed, doors that open, furniture and objects moving across the floor and through the air, footsteps, the smell of corpses, the smell of baby powder, growling sounds, and having your hair pulled, to name a few. Basically, enough paranormal activity has been reported to fill an entire book, or two.

If you recall, at the beginning of this story I alluded to my unpleasant experiences at the mental hospital, and Lori and Kirk both related experiences that reinforced the fact that places of death and suffering such as this were not for the faint of heart—or lungs.

Kirk told of one woman who felt as if a plastic bag had been pulled down over her head and she couldn't breathe. Panicked, she ran from the area and, to her relief, found that she could breath again with no problem. Fifteen minutes later she returned to the same spot and again could not catch her breath.

While conducting a tour through the tuberculosis ward one day, Lori stepped into room #29 and was suddenly overcome with an excruciating pain that felt as if her spine was being crushed. Despite the crippling pain, she was concerned that the people on the tour would think this was all some part of an act, but they quickly realized her agony was genuine.

Lori sensed that the spirit of a woman who had died of tuberculosis was showing her what it was really like to succumb to that terrible disease. Fortunately, after a minute or so, the pain ceased as quickly as it had overcome her. Shocked from the awful experience, but still curious, Lori did some research because she had thought that TB only affected the lungs. She discovered that the disease could strike many parts of the body and victims did indeed suffer very painful deaths. Later, Lori let the spirit know that her message had been received loud and clear, and to please never cause that pain again!

The tour had been very enlightening and in addition to the stories, we had heard enough inexplicable noises and felt enough odd feelings to be optimistic that our investigation could get very interesting. We went back to the café where our cases of equipment were stacked up, and began to formulate our plan for the night. The idea was to leave camcorders and audio recorders in several of the paranormal hotspots, and then slowly go through every wing, hallway and corridor and see what we could find.

There were many sounds throughout the night, and it would be impossible to state that every one was of paranormal origin. However, a few were so close and so loud that we could rule out most natural explanations. Each time we tried to find a source, but in each case the only conclusion we could reach was that the source was unknown, and suspiciously paranormal.

One such instance occurred in the nurses' quarters. There was a very loud knocking sound within a few feet of us. We immediately aimed our flashlights in the direction of the sound, but found nothing that could have caused it. A few moments later, there were sounds behind Mike, as if someone was coming up behind him. Again, we all quickly turned but couldn't see anything.

I have to point out that from my perspective, everything that had happened so far was interesting, but not frightening or intimidating, which was all pleasantly surprising. Even when I walked into the morgue and there was a metallic sound like something hitting a pipe, I was intrigued, but not scared. I mention this now not to claim any great bravery on my part, but to emphasize the general atmosphere as I perceived it, and my state of mind. This will be important when I explain events that occurred later on, and their sharp contrast to what I had experienced previously.

As we navigated the maze of hallways, we came to one of the long, dank, underground tunnels. Again, there were sounds all around us in the darkness, and although the air was a cool 64 degrees, at one point an icy chill swept over us. Mike and I pulled out our infrared non-contact thermometers like a pair of gunslingers in a quick draw, and found that the temperature had dropped to 44 degrees. You might expect a variation of several degrees in any location, but a sharp, instantaneous drop of twenty degrees is not normal. And as I have said on numerous occassions, there's something about a genuine paranormal cold spot that goes right through you and often makes your hair stand on end. This was one of those cases where instinct and experience said that we were not alone in that tunnel.

The Christmas Room was interesting. We set up some equipment there, and before we left we got several high EMF readings. We also placed some toys along some lines and photographed them, but unfortunately when we returned we found that they had not moved. But that room did not disappoint us.

Marge and I were alone in the Christmas Room later on, and I was taking some infrared photos. There was a radio-controlled car sitting on the floor and I challenged any spirits who might be there to move the car. Nothing happened and I turned my attention elsewhere. Then Marge started saying, "Look! Look at the car antenna!"

Turning back, by the light of her flashlight I saw that the long wire antenna was whipping back and forth. The car itself hadn't moved, but something had caused the antenna to move dramatically. This wasn't a barely detectable quivering that might be caused by the vibrations of our footsteps—that antenna was swinging as if someone had pulled it down and let it go. Impressive!

The basement tunnel where we experienced the cold spot. Remember, we moved about in darkness, and the camera flash definitely detracts from the spooky appearance.

When the four of us checked out the level that contained the shops, Mike and Marge told me about the bad feelings they had experienced by the model railroad room right after we had first arrived. They again encountered the same disturbing sensations by that room. In addition, we all heard banging sounds coming from the solarium at the end of the hall. We hurried down there, but as soon as we entered the room, the sounds stopped. A pattern was clearly developing here...

The Christmas Room.

A few minutes before midnight, we started to investigate the east wing, which was the ladies' ward when it was only a home for the elderly. Almost immediately, we heard footsteps over our heads, and assumed that members of the RHGHS were on the floor above us. Then we remembered that on our tour, Lori and Kirk had said there was no other floor above that wing, just the roof. The door to the roof was kept locked and no one had been up there for years.

Despite that, many other people had reported hearing footsteps that were so clear and distinct that they also just assumed another group of people was above them, and then were stunned to find that wasn't possible. And let me assure you, these were not the sounds of animals—unless they weighed over one hundred and fifty pounds, stood upright and wore hard-soled shoes! (That would be one bunch of squirrels I wouldn't want to mess with!)

As we began to slowy make our way down the corridor, with the sounds of footsteps above us, there was a sharp sound from the solarium at the end of the hall. I won't say this was getting monotonous—clearly not a word to be used while standing in a dark ayslum at midnight!—but it wasn't anything we hadn't heard before.

I still wasn't experiencing any anxiety at this point, but Marge was obviously feeling otherwise. She suddenly announced that this wing was too uncomfortable for her and she left, saying she would wait for us in the cafe. Just after she left there were more noises from the solarium, and Mike, Scott and I continued on toward the sounds.

Soon after we began to move again, there was a perceptible shift in the atmosphere. Nothing strong, but definitely noticeable, and of the nature of which I can best describe as being "confrontational." In fact, at that moment I said, "I feel like we are walking into a gunfight." There were the three of us, equipment in hand, walking in line down the long hallway toward sounds we could not explain, about to face what, we didn't know. It was like some bizarre paranormal western, and little did I realize that the bad guys were planning an ambush...

A bit further down the hall Mike asked if anyone wanted to make their presence known. Again it sounded like several people were walking just over our heads. Then a sound came from about forty feet ahead of us. Then there were banging and tapping sounds behind us which caused us to stop and listen quietly, and Mike commented that there were "sounds all around us."

Next a tapping sound could be heard in a room near where Mike was standing, and he felt compelled to go inside. A few moments later he came out and exclaimed, "Oh, Jesus!"

"Not good?" I asked, knowing full well that whatever he had just experienced in that room would have sent most people running and screaming.

"Covered in goose bumps," he replied, then took a moment before he explained what had happened.

As soon as he entered the room, there was a banging sound directly above him and noises all along the wall next to him, not to mention a horrible, overwhelming feeling. We checked for a number over the doorway and I half expected that it would be room #29, where Lori had experienced the pain of a woman who had died of TB. I was half right—while it wasn't the doorway that read #29, it was a doorway at the other end of the large double room. So it was in fact, that same room where something very bad happens to sensitive people.

The ladies' wing, were arguably the most unpleasant encounters occur.

We finally made it to the solarium and sure enough, the sounds emanating from that room ceased as soon as we crossed the threshold. In a way, I was relieved that there wasn't a powerful confrontation, but on the other hand I was there for direct evidence of a haunting, not a cat and mouse game of follow the bouncing sounds. We stood in the silent darkness for a while, then Mike shouted, "If anyone is hear, respond by making a noise."

On cue, another heavy banging sound echoed down the hallway we had just come down.

"*That* was a noise," I stated with some satisfaction.

"That was definitely a noise," Mike said, similarly pleased by the instant response.

We waited a while longer in the solarium to see if anything else might happen there, but persistent sounds back down the hallway made it clear that the scene of the action had shifted once again. As I left the solarium, I again noted that I was perfectly calm, and except for Marge's departure, the investigation had progressed in an orderly and scientific fashion. Let me tell you, enjoy that feeling while you can on a ghost hunt, because everything can change in one terrifying heartbeat!

As we made our way back down the hall, the noises began again behind us, and continued in front of us, as well. In the darkness, I hadn't realized that I had gotten about ten or twelve feet ahead of Mike and Scott, and all of a sudden as I approached a doorway to my left, an awful, threatening presence rushed out. I couldn't see it, I couldn't hear it, but I felt it as surely as if someone had run into me.

I have been in prisons, cemeteries, murder and suicide scenes and have experienced all manner of negative entities, but rarely have I felt personally endangered. At that shocking moment, not only did I feel threatened, but it was a tangible feeling that this entity hated women, and was threatening me on a profoundly personal level. I had never expereinced that sensation before—at least not from the dead—and I felt the overwhelming need to move between Mike and Scott. This all happened in a split second, and I felt that I would be safer if I could get in the middle of the two men.

Get in the middle, must get in the middle, I thought to myself.

I quickly moved between Mike and Scott, and actually felt shielded by their male energy. Believe me, as I write this now, I know it sounds crazy, but at that moment it was like a survival instinct kicked in. I have never been one who felt the need to seek protection from men, but I'm not too proud to say that under the circumstances I did what I felt I had to do. I didn't have time to explain what was going on, and I had only started to say that I was feeling uncomfortable when Mike spoke.

"Did you ever play that game with a baseball where you're in the middle and you're trying to run to each base?" he asked as my jaw dropped when he said "middle."

"Monkey in Middle," Scott said.

"That's how I feel right now," Mike continued.

What's that expression, that you could knock me over with a feather? Despite the fear of the moment, I was astonished.

"Well, look at what I just did," I said, gesturing with my arms to indicate how I had moved into the middle of the two of them. "I stood right between you two because I didn't feel safe."

"They've got us between them," Mike stated calmly as if observing a chess match.

"I can't *believe* you said that!" I said with considerably less calm. Despite feeling somewhat protected in the middle of the two men, the threatening presence—or was it two?—was still right there with us, within arm's length. As I took a breath and tried to relax, it felt like more than one negative entity wanted a piece of me. That was it, and evidence or not, I had enough.

"I'm getting the hell out of here," I said as I hurried to the heavy double doors at the end of the hallway. Fortunately, as soon as I passed through the doors, the terrible sensation stopped.

They can't reach me out here, I thought, greatly relieved.

Mike and Scott soon exited, and Mike explained how he felt that whoever was in there had maneuvered us to that particular location.

"They moved us there with the noises," he concluded, as I thought back to how we kept moving in response to the sounds around us.

"Okay, that's a keeper!" I declared, regaining more of my controlled ghost investigator demeanor. But I couldn't help adding, "But I didn't like that!"

Now that several weeks have passed and I have had a chance to review all of the tapes and video, and I've written about the incident, I'm probably even more impressed—and not necessarily in a good way!—by that experience. Throughout that night I had been curious, but not anxious, alert, but not frightened, until the "attack" in that hallway. It was one of the most startling, intense and upsetting events in my ghost hunting career.

I just spoke about the investigation during a lecture a few nights ago, and even then the scene came back to me as if it had just happened. I wish there had been some supporting evidence (two semi-solid apparitions swirling around me on video would have been nice), but I only have my own personal experiences and vivid memories to show for it. As always, I would suggest that you find out for yourself what this hallway is like, as well as the remaining 65,000 square feet, by visiting Rolling Hills and conducting your own investigation. Just be prepared—especially you ladies—for something powerful and hostile.

We made our way back to the café where Marge was relaxing. I told her she had made the smart move by leaving that wing right away. I wanted to ask Lori about that area, but I didn't want to immediately say what I had experienced. Never pose a question like, "Did you see that blue elephant in the back right corner of the green room?" Instead, simply ask, "Have there been any unusual sightings in the green room, and if so, in what part of the room?" It's not that I don't think witnesses are honest, but I would prefer to remove the possibility of the power of suggestion.

When I found Lori, I only said I had an interesting experience in that particular wing, and asked what others had reported there. The first words out of her mouth were startling, but not totally unexpected.

"The angry spirits of two men who hate women are in that wing, and a lot of women have felt threatened by them."

Good thing there weren't any feathers around, because you could have knocked me over once again. I then told her what had happened to me, and she related details of similar incidents reported by other women. As unpleasant as it had been, this was exactly the reason I spend long hours in creepy places, looking for evidence such as this. I checked the audio of our tour when we first arrived, and no one had mentiond the two threatening male entities. There was no way I could have known about them beforehand. Marge felt them, then I felt them, and Lori confirmed that we certainly weren't the first, and most likely won't be the last.

Even the skeptics among you must admit this is pushing the limits of a mere coincidence!

After a well-deserved break, Mike, Scott and I headed back into the fray. The room where the terrible electroshock treatements took place was fascinating. We each stood in a different corner, and I guess I was the lucky one because right away I felt my right arm tingling, there was a buzzing in my right ear and I felt a little lightheaded. Fortunately, this time there wasn't anything scary or threatening, at least. Still, it wasn't pleasant and I suggested that Mike and I switch places to see if he felt anything.

The sensation stopped as soon as I moved across the room. When Mike stepped into that corner, he rather imprudently shouted, "Don't pick on Linda! If you're going to pick on someone, pick on me!" There was a short pause, then he added, "*What* did I just say!?" as he realized the implications of his challenge. We all had a good laugh over it, but that didn't make the bad feelings in that corner subside. In fact, they intensified as Mike was suddenly engulfed in a bone-chilling mass of cold air. He, too, decided to move away from that area.

Be very careful what you ask for, especially in a haunted asylum!

There was a banging noise out in the hall, loud enough to be picked up by the digital recorder I carried. That was almost immediately followed by a sound coming from the adjoining room. Mike and I went inside, and encountered a very bad feeling, almost painful, and Mike also started feeling something brushing across his head. We aimed the flashlights in his direction, but there were no webs, strings or anything hanging from the ceiling. Still, the feeling persisted even as Mike moved his hands back and forth over his scalp to try to stop whatever was casuing the unnerving sensation. We finally had to leave that room.

Mike enters the adjoining room in the electroshock treatment area just after we heard a noise.

We continued on through countless rooms and corridors. Several times there were banging, crashing and tapping sounds in the darkness before us, or behind us, and while we didn't exactly get used to the paranormal sound effects, we came to accept them as part of the territory. When we found ourselves back at the infamous second floor east wing, where Mike wanted to set up some equipment, I was hesitant to step back inside, even for a few minutes.

Don't be a baby, I thought to myself as I crossed over the threshold. While the threatening feeling wasn't as intense, it was most definitely still there, and I kept close to Mike and Scott as we set up a camcorder and some meters. I was quite relieved to exit that wing, and decided it was the last time I would go in there that night.

Scott and Mike set up a camcorder in the ladies' wing. The area where I experienced the "attack" is ahead on the right.

We eventually made our way back to the café. It was getting very late at this point, and fatigue was beginning to get the better of me. I decided to start packing up, while Mike and Scott headed back to the dreaded wing to retrieve the equipment—and see if they could stir things up even more. We remained in contact over the walkie-talkies, which was as close as I cared to get to that terrible place.

They both experienced an oppressive feeling upon entering, but not threatening. After going a short distance they heard a sharp sound as if something was dropped in one of the rooms near them. Mike thought it was to their left, and also thought he saw something moving across the floor. Scott thought the sound came from the room to their right. Perhaps it was hard to distinguish the source due to echoes, or perhaps, as Mike commented, "They're playing with us again."

They continued down to the end of the long hallway, at which point a heavy pounding could be heard behind them. Mike then realized it was a long way back to the exit doors—through the gamut of unnerving sounds and angry spirits—and expressed his dismay in some colorful language!

The noises continued around them—including a distinct clinking sound like something striking a lightbulb—as they cautiously made their way back in the darkness. When they returned to the equipment they had set up by the exit, Mike decided to have a few parting words with the inhospitable inhabitants. It defintely made for interesting listening several days later when I heard the recording of those twenty minutes they spent in that wing. Mike really gave them a piece of his mind, which was some small satisfaction for me, having had such a rough time there.

Calling the spirits cowards, telling them they were afraid to come out and were only capable of scaring women, were just a few of his remarks. After a few minutes of this entity-scolding, he offered another challenge—daring the spirits to come out and face men for change, unless they were too afraid. Scott also added his two cents about the cowardice of the women-hating ghosts. A moment later waves of goosbumps swept over Mike, and both he and Scott felt a shift in the atmosphere. Loud banging noises echoed down the hall, and footsteps appeared to be headed their way.

"Uh-oh!" Mike said, realizing that he might have rattled the wrong paranormal cages.

The footsteps continued to approach them from somewhere down the hall, although nothing could be seen and the phantom walker never reached them. However, the opressive feeling grew in intensity and it had became quite uncomfortable. It was beginning to look like an excellent time to end the investigation and leave! The matter was settled for them when the RHGHS group arrived on the scene. They planned to investigate that wing, and Mike and Scott were certainly not averse to the idea of turning the location over to the group, now that they had irritated all the spirits!

As we packed up our equipment, we all agreed it had been an amazing night. There would be a lot of video and audio to go through in the following days, and a lot of experiences to personally process. First, however, was the small matter of a 300 mile trip home. I was physically and emotionally drained, but also wired, so I could only manage a few ten minute naps here and there. Fortunately, Mike's years of night shifts with the police, and lots of coffee, kept him awake.

It is always strange driving in darkness and then slowly watching the landscape brighten. As the sun climbed over the horizon and full daylight was upon us, it was hard to believe that just hours earlier we were in the pitch blackness of a haunted asylum, being threatened by things long dead.

On my drive home from Port Jervis through the morning rush hour traffic, it was all a very surreal, disconnected feeling. After all we had been through while all these people had slept, and now they all went about their lives, oblivious to what fate may await them if they lead unfilled lives…

Okay, I was really, *really*, tired, and was just getting too philosophical, I guess…

Rather than pondering the eternal fate of mankind, what I really needed to do was get home, take a hot shower and go to sleep for about a week.

Of course, curiosity got the better of me and a few hours later I was up and started reviewing the photos, video and audio. It gave me chills to watch and hear the "monkey in the middle" encounter again, and see the long, dark corridors that held so many frightening mysteries. It had been one of my most emotionally challenging investigations—not to mention physically exhausting—and after days of reviewing evidence I came to one inalterable conclusion:

I had to go back.

I had to face the evil of the second floor again.

Four Months Later

I don't appreciate being intimidated.

As a ghost investigator who confronts the unknown on a regular basis, it's important to be able to deal with just about anything the sprit world dishes out. So when I had the unpleasant experience at the Rolling Hills Asylum that caused me to retreat from the second floor east wing, I was irritated—irritated at myself for being vulnerable, but more so at the SOBs (Spirits Obnoxious and Belligerent) who had gotten under my skin.

I needed to go back and face them.

The opportunity arose with the first annual "Ghoststock" in July 2006—a unique gathering of ghost hunters from across the country, who would spend the weekend investigating at night and attending presentations during the day. Lori invited me to be one of the speakers and I looked forward to presenting some of my most interesting cases to people who have experience in the field. I also welcomed the chance to confront my fears. This time they wouldn't catch me off guard. I would be prepared. (At least I hoped so!)

Mike and I set out for the asylum on a hot and humid Friday morning. Apart from one blinding downpour, the trip went smoothly and we arrived at our hotel just at check-in time. Unfortunately, the rooms weren't ready yet, so rather than waiting around we decided to get back on the road and shoot up to Niagara Falls, which is only about forty minutes away. However, as we hadn't eaten a meal all day and we knew the falls would still be falling later on, we first headed to the Seneca Indian casino for their massive buffet.

As a vegetarian, I'm always pessimistic about what choices I will have in any restaurant, let alone in a casino filled with carnivorous gamblers. To my delight, however, there was a huge selection of delicious veggie items. Everything was so good I was too full to even finish my chocolate cake for dessert—which is more shocking and unusual than seeing a ghost! As Mike and I rolled out of the buffet, we both hoped that our overindulgence wasn't going to come back to haunt us...

We then walked off some of our dinner along the falls where the sites are so spectacular I never tire of seeing them. Unfortunately, a nasty thunderstorm was poised to cross the border from Canada, so we didn't stay as long as we would have liked. We finally checked into our hotel, and if our timing had been a little off and we were too early at the first attempt, it was perfect timing the second time. The people who checked in right in front us became trapped in the elevator when it broke down. They were in the hot, crowded elevator for well over an hour, which is one experience I was glad to miss. There were enough stressful situations awaiting me that night.

Okay, so this has nothing to do with ghosts, but I couldn't resist including it. While walking along the falls, I wondered why a crowd of people were looking down at the ground, rather than looking out at the spectacular scenery. Then I saw they were looking at this lucky squirrel having the time of his life with a discarded ice cream cone. (That's vanilla ice cream on his nose.)

As there were over a hundred and twenty-five ghost hunters attending Ghoststock, investigation times had to be scheduled. Mike and I were in the midnight slot for the east wing, which seemed like a fitting time. There would be several other groups in that wing at the same time, so as everyone else seemed to be beginning in the basement, Mike and I dashed up the stairs to have some time alone with our old "acquaintances" there.

Imagine this in the dark—you go through double doors and the hallway angles to the right. Do those other doors lead to rooms, stairs, another hallway, or all of the above? And where are those sounds coming from, and what could be lurking around the corner?

I have to reiterate how disorienting this place is, especially in the dark. We were fairly sure we had found the right hallway, and were fairly sure we were headed up the right staircase. I didn't become certain until we faced the closed metal door to the infamous wing. Scientific or not, I could just *feel* that this was the place, and that something was lurking on the other side.

Taking a deep breath, I stepped inside and said out loud, "I'm back." I wanted to let them know I was onto their game, and they weren't going to surprise me this time.

Although nothing immediately rushed out of the darkness at me, I was on high alert and was not going to let my guard down for one second. I was also not going to let Mike get too far from me.

As he moved ahead to set up some equipment, I said, "Ohhhh, no you don't," and then hurried to keep up with him. I may have been prepared, but it never hurts to have backup.

We took a minute or so to power up all the equipment, then slowly started making our way down the corridor. I did my best to make myself aware of the difference between my expectations and the reality of the situation. It's an ability everyone possesses, but I think after a decade of ghost hunting, that ability to discriminate between the two becomes more refined.

It had better be if you want to be a good ghost investigator! It would not serve me well if my imagination controlled these situations. So as intense or frightening as things may get, I need to keep a handle on my fears and determine what is created internally, and what is from an external paranormal source.

There was no doubt that the sounds we began hearing all around us were definitely from an external source! What that source was, however, remained to be seen—and I mean that literally. At one point I turned toward the direction of a sound, and it clearly looked like there was a dark figure standing in a doorway about thirty feet away.

The image appeared for several seconds, and then it was gone. I told Mike what I had seen and I tried to reproduce the figure with my flashlight and infrared camcorder. I thought perhaps some kind of reflected light might have cast the roughly six-foot-tall shadow at the edge of doorway, but I couldn't reproduce it. Lori later told me that recently there had been several sightings of "shadow beings" on this floor.

A minute later, Mike and I both commented that the atmosphere was "oppressive" and "heavy." There was a loud bang over our heads, and Mike's fully charged camcorder battery registered only eleven minutes of available power, and then died, all in the span of about ten seconds.

The situation was escalating quickly.

"I feel like I'm being watched," Mike whispered as he replaced the dead battery.

I agreed. It wasn't something you could measure scientifically, but you would have to be completely oblivious not to feel it.

Not ten seconds later, there was a very loud banging/scraping sound from somewhere down the corridor in front of us. The unusual noise was loud enough to be picked up on the audio recorder, as was Mike's reaction—which will not be reprinted here due to the nature of the language (but I'm sure you can easily figure it out!). I replied that I had no idea what that could have been, and we stood perfectly still in the darkness, waiting to see what would happen next.

As I write this now, having just listened to the recording again and again, I am even more impressed by the sound. It was like some heavy wooden or metal object hit the floor and was then dragged. At the time I described it as "weird," as I could not imagine what could have made such a bizarre slamming, banging, twisted sound. There is no way this could have been produced naturally—especially considering the fact that we were the only two people on that floor.

As we were trying to absorb the startling noise, something else made another sound behind us (a much softer bang or tap). I turned around to see if anything was behind us, but Mike was still facing the direction of the loud sound, and he suddenly whispered, "There's something moving down there!"

I turned back, but it was too late for me to see the dark figure that he saw moving quickly across the hallway near the solarium. You can imagine how tense the situation was—it was very dark, an incredibly loud banging sound had just echoed down the hallway, we had both seen shadowy figures, and we had no idea what might come at us at any given second. I guarantee that most sane people would be running for their cars at this point.

However, after taking a deep breath I said with conviction, "Well, I suppose we have to go down there."

We started moving cautiously, but deliberately, toward the solarium, and with every step the number of goose bumps increased across my body. It not only felt like someone was in front of us, and behind us, it also felt as if someone was above us. Monkey in the middle, and on top…

Then Mike's new camcorder battery went dead, making two drained batteries in the span of just a few minutes. A moment later, he inadvertently kicked a chair that we couldn't see in the blackness and we both almost jumped out of our skin. (The words we said will also not be reprinted here, but you can easily figure them out. Comments made at moments like these are rarely eloquent.)

Checking each room as we moved down the corridor, we finally made it to the solarium and were able to confirm that we were indeed alone on this floor. Any figures we had seen, any sounds we had heard and recorded, were definitely not from the world of the living.

We sat on the floor of the solarium for a few minutes, and there was a noticeable shift in the atmosphere. The tension had dissipated, and it felt fairly normal, under the circumstances. It seemed that whatever negative entities lurked in that wing were limited to the corridor and rooms on either side. It was somehow a comforting thought—if there were evil ghosts, they had boundaries, which meant their power was limited.

Unfortunately, our time on that floor was also limited, as a couple of minutes later we heard footsteps and saw lights at the far end of the wing. Another team of ghost hunters was entering, which probably meant the end of our investigation here.

First Rule of Ghost Hunting: The reliability of evidence is inversely proportional to the number of ghost hunters!

But it was okay, and probably for the best, because realistically I'm not certain how much more strain our nerves could have taken. As you sit there and read this, hopefully you get some sense of what happened, but mere words cannot convey the feeling of being in the dark with noises and shadowy figures and an electricity in the air that sends chills up your spine.

We started walking toward the other group, and as a professional courtesy Mike was going to let them know what had been going on. However, these ghost hunters were obviously on a mission, and blew right by us with no acknowledgement.

Laughing softly, I said to Mike, "Okay, I guess they don't want to have anything to do with us."

A few moments later they began speaking out loud their list of EVP questions (asking a series of questions, then later checking the recording for any response), so that definitely signaled the end of our quiet time on this floor. As were we leaving, more people arrived, and we spoke to them and compared notes.

There was one final tense moment as I looked through my infrared camcorder and clearly saw the shadow of a man on a file cabinet in the hallway. There was no visible light source to cast a shadow, and for a brief second I thought it was the real deal—until I saw the shadow was wearing shorts!

Checking behind us, I saw through my camcorder that the EVPers had an infrared light (invisible to the naked eye), which was casting a shadow of Mike against the file cabinet. Oh well, a little comedy relief helped dissolve the tension of the past twenty minutes.

As it seemed as though everyone was headed upstairs, we went down. In one of the lower level rooms we heard some kind of movement along one of the walls. Mike shined his flashlight in that direction as I asked him if he thought it was, "Animal or vegetable...or spirit?" We were unable to find anything that might have made the odd sound.

We found our way back to the auditorium/recreation room and sat quietly in the darkness on the end of the stage for a while. There was an uneasy feeling to this room, and after several minutes Mike began asking some questions. There was no response until he asked, "Did you come to this room and have happy times?"

A brief moment passed, then in an urgent tone he said, "Something is touching my back, Linda. Something is touching my lower back!"

I turned on the camcorder and swung around to see if anything was visible, but it was not. All I could see was Mike placing his hand on his back and saying, "It was here, it was going down my back."

"Like a hand?" I asked.

"Like a finger. At first I tried to ignore it...oh, my God..."

"Still there?" I asked, thinking he still felt the phantom finger running down his back.

The feeling of the finger had passed, but he was being overwhelmed with emotion. He managed to explain that he tried to ignore it, but the finger kept pushing harder, and then started tracing a line down his back. Even more disturbing, it felt like the finger of a child.

After taking a deep breath, Mike added, "It upset me."

That was obviously a huge understatement by the look on his face. He explained that he felt great sadness, and it was as if some spirit was trying to communicate that there *were no* happy times in this place. The message came through loud and clear.

We sat for a few more minutes until we heard another group headed our way. We could have moved to another location, but the episode had completely drained Mike, and I was a bit wasted myself. We decided we had enough emotional trauma for one night.

Of course, trying to fall asleep after such experiences is not easy. Your mind replays everything, and you try to piece together all of the bizarre things you just encountered. I did manage a few hours of sleep, but unfortunately was wide-awake early the next morning.

My presentation wasn't scheduled until 2pm, but we headed back to the asylum early to have another look around in daylight. I could see that at first it was uncomfortable for Mike to go back into the auditorium after that terrible encounter with the finger on his back. Even in the heat and bright sunlight the place gave me a chill.

I had been looking forward to presenting some of my most interesting cases to fellow ghost hunters, and indeed it was a pleasure speaking to a group who knew what it was really like to experience a haunting firsthand. Until you have come face to face with something from the other world, you just can't fully appreciate the impact it has on you. Whether or not that's a good thing is another matter...

Beginning my presentation in the auditorium just a few feet from where Mike was touched by a child's finger the night before.

I was thoroughly fried by the time I arrived back home that night—physically, mentally and emotionally. People who think such trips are like vacations don't quite get it. But hey, if I wanted rest and relaxation, I wouldn't drive 600 miles to spend the night in a haunted asylum!

Given all we have been through, will I even consider going back? Absolutely! This is a genuinely haunted place from top to bottom, with more mysteries to unravel than you can imagine. For those of you who are looking to get your paranormal feet wet in your first ghost hunt, this would be an excellent place to start. Just be prepared for encounters that may not be pleasant, to say the least.

With all of the attention now being focused on the spirits of the Rolling Hills Asylum, perhaps it will somehow ease their suffering and help them to move on. It's bad enough these poor souls had to spend their lives here…

If you want to experience Rolling Hills for yourself, the website and phone number are below. Just tell them the Ghost Investigator sent you, and good luck!

http://www.rollinghills-ghosthunt.com/
585-344-2888

Ghost Briefs

Since my last book, I've had quite a few ghost hunting adventures, given many lectures, done several TV and radio shows, and received tons of email that I haven't always had the time to respond to—sorry! I think the next year will prove to be just as fascinating as I have an ever-growing list of cases to investigate. There is no shortage of the restless dead!

One case that has drawn a lot of interest is *Body in the Basement?* from *Ghost Investigator Volume 5*, where there very well may be the skeletal remains of a boy who haunts a Monroe, NY home. I was determined to try to dig for these bones, and one day with the owner's permission, and assistance, we gave it a try.

As the exposed section of dirt basement was in a very confined area with a low ceiling, we could only work in a sitting position. We donned Tyvek suits and filter masks to try to keep from getting completely filthy and breathing in decades of god-knows-what.

Unfortunately, to further complicate matters, the ground was incredibly hard and compact, and what looked to be a few hours of digging turned into a long day of chiseling and scraping at the rock-like soil to even make a dent. Without something like a small jackhammer, it would be extremely difficult to get down five or six feet. The other problem is the structural integrity of the foundation walls. If all that supporting soil is removed, would the walls collapse?

It's all very frustrating, because the haunting continues, and there have now been several independent psychics who believe bones are somewhere under that house. Perhaps some day the truth will be uncovered...

For those of you who think it's glamorous being an author and ghost investigator let me assure you it can be a very dirty business—especially when digging for bodies. Here I am taking a breather from the back-breaking work of searching for human remains in an old basement.

Around Halloween in 2005, I spent the day shooting a story on Hudson Valley ghosts for Cablevision. It was a long day, but it was fun visiting some "old haunts." We shot in quite a few locations that day, and two of my favorite places were the Mansion Restaurant in Pearl River, NY (story in *GI V1*) and the Old '76 House in Tappan, NY (story in *GI V4*). Both places have great food and "spirits."

Here I am on the beautiful main staircase of the Mansion Restaurant. The place contains a Tiffany window, fine woodwork, and at least one mischievous ghost of a former resident who has been seen on these stairs.

The Old '76 House is famous for its history and ghosts—and one of the most active spots seems to be Table #2 which is directly behind my right shoulder. Be sure to ask for that table when making reservations if you're looking for an out-of-this-world dining experience!

A lot of my cases first come to my attention when I give lectures. People in the audience share their personal stories, as well as suggest other possible haunted locations in the area. I really appreciate this information, as it has led to many amazing experiences.

Below is a photo taken at the Merritt Bookstore in Millbrook, NY, (a great independent bookstore) where I've spoken in October for the last several years. I'm in the back behind the crowd, listening to stories and hoping to learn of a few more good haunts.

Last, and certainly not least, is the ongoing story of Grandma's House in Port Jervis. We had a very interesting investigation there one night with many of Mike's relatives in attendance.

It was an unusual setup—all of his relatives gathered in the kitchen around a monitor that was hooked up to a camcorder upstairs. This way they were able to watch what was going on as Mike and I went from room to room. There were some angry banging sounds, a shadowy figure, and a night filled with bizarre sights, sounds and feelings.

The activity here actually seems to be on the increase, perhaps because Mike's young twin boys are very sensitive. They often describe seeing people and figures in the house, and can describe them in great detail. What they can't understand is why none of the adults can see them! They also recently said that there were ghosts in the wall where something responded to my tapping. Of all the places in the house to pick, the boys identified that exact spot!

This is one case where year after year there's been no cessation of activity, and there always seems to be something new. Unfortunately, some of the encounters have been terrifying this past year, as there is a definite shift toward the negative end of the spiritual spectrum.

We will continue to search for answers, and see if it's possible to clear this house once and for all. Stay tuned…

To order books, get info, and share your haunting, contact the Ghost Investigator through:

www.ghostinvestigator.com

Or write to:

Linda Zimmermann
P.O. Box 192
Blooming Grove, NY 10914

Or send email to:

linda@gotozim.com

Copy this page to use for your own ghost hunt. If you know of a haunted site you think should be considered for an upcoming book, please contact me at:
P.O. Box 192, Blooming Grove, NY, 10914
www.ghostinvestigator.com

Field Report

Date: **Location:**

Time In: **Weather:**

Names of People Interviewed:

Equipment: Camera ☐ **Video** ☐ **Tape Recorder** ☐
Thermometer ☐ **Other:**

Experiences: Sounds ☐ **Odors** ☐ **Cold Spots** ☐
Visuals ☐ **Touch/Sensations** ☐ **Movement** ☐

Details (Attach extra sheet if necessary):

Time Out: **Total Time on Site:**

Conclusions:

Prepared and Signed by:

Witness(es):

Other books by Linda Zimmermann

Ghost Hunter Novel

Dead Center

When one of the country's largest shopping centers is built in Virginia, rumors abound that the place is haunted by ghosts of Civil War soldiers. Ghost hunter Sarah Brooks must uncover the truth, and come face to face with the restless spirits that walk through the *Dead Center* :

Okay, Sarah Brooks. This is what you do, she said to herself. *This is who you are.*
Closing her eyes, Sarah spun around and counted to three. When she opened her eyes, she had to clamp her hand over her mouth to stifle a scream. There was a pale, misty shape of a man drawing closer. It was like an image being projected into a fog, and it rippled, wavered, then slowly began to take on a more defined shape. The wounded man behind her screamed as if Death himself was coming to take him…

Science Fiction Novels

Mind Over Matter

Ten wealthy, powerful members of the Upper Circle rule the Union with an iron fist, and a small chip implanted in every citizen. Born to the privileged class, Walter Danan is now a wanted man. He has discovered extraordinary powers with which he hopes to break the council's grip and set mankind on a higher path of *Mind Over Matter*.

"Classic space opera!" Ernest Lilley, Editor, *SFRevu*

Home Run

On the fast track to becoming a baseball superstar, Rick Stella's injury leads him to join the Pioneer program for a year-long mission. Pioneers are sent into the farthest depths of space to start colonies, and are often never heard from again.

When Rick becomes marooned with his android crew, he must decide whether he is willing to sacrifice his dreams, or risk everything trying to make it home.

"Linda Zimmermann shows why she's an All-star in combining a story about baseball & SF to remind us how to overcome obstacles to emerge a winner!" Tony Tellado, *Sci-Fi Talk*

History

Civil War Memories "An exciting compilation of vignettes which bring Civil War history alive." Alan Aimone, USMA West Point

Forging a Nation "Linda Zimmermann blends the history of a single family with the history of our nation in its formative years. This is a story of patriotism, privilege and tragedy which touches the heart, and gives the reader a fascinating and very personal window into the past."
William E. Simon, former U.S. Secretary of the Treasury

"A worthy book." Arthur Schlesinger, Pulitzer Prize winning author/historian

www.ingramcontent.com/pod-product-compliance
Ingram Content Group UK Ltd.
Pitfield, Milton Keynes, MK11 3LW, UK
UKHW041426180426
11947UKWH00007B/316